THEATRICAL DIGS

THEATRICAL DIGS

Tales From The Green Room

FEATURING

the illustrious members of

The Lord's Taverners' Company

A GRAHAM TARRANT BOOK

DAVID & CHARLES

Newton Abbot   London   North Pomfret (Vt)

The Lord's Taverners and the Publishers gratefully acknowledge permission to quote from the following works:
My Farce from My Elbow by Brian Rix, published by Secker & Warburg; *A Touch of the Memoirs* by Donald Sinden, published by Hodder & Stoughton; *Twice Brightly* by Harry Secombe, published by Robson Books; *Morecambe and Wife* by Joan Morecambe, published by Pelham Books.

British Library Cataloguing in Publication Data

Theatrical digs: tales from the green room.
—— (A Graham Tarrant book).
1. Theatre   2. Actors – Correspondence,
reminiscences, etc.   2. Authors –
Correspondence, reminiscences, etc.
I. Lord's Taverners
792'.092'2   PN2020

ISBN 0–7153–8982–3

Typeset by Northern Phototypesetting Co, Bolton
and printed in Great Britain
by Billings Ltd Worcester
for David & Charles Publishers plc
Brunel House Newton Abbot Devon

Published in the United States of America
by David & Charles Inc
North Pomfret Vermont 05053 USA

Contents

CONTENTS

Illustrations by Gren Jones, Bill Tidy, Colin Whittock

The Lord's Taverners

THE Lord's Taverners began life in 1950 outside the Tavern at Lord's Cricket Ground. The Tavern was the gathering place for 'cricketing actors and acting cricketers'. In those pre-TV days, curtain-up was not until 8pm, thereby enabling the actor to watch cricket until close of play.

There were some illustrious names among the early members – John Mills, Richard Attenborough, Jack Hawkins, Peter Sellers, Laurence Olivier, Richard Burton, and a host of others. The early membership was truly from the stage and world of entertainment or, as we now call it, show biz. The businessman joined later to assist with the administration, but the charity was founded by thespians for thespians. Nothing pleased the actor more than to play cricket with the likes of Len Hutton or Freddie Trueman. The cricketer was equally thrilled to be playing alongside stars of the stage and screen.

With the advent of television the 'celebrity' arrived and The Lord's Taverners' membership received famous names like Terry Wogan, Jimmy Tarbuck, Bruce Forsyth, Harry Secombe, Morecambe and Wise, and many more.

The 'celebrity' is the backbone of the modern Taverners. He or she makes a number of personal appearances on our behalf – giving away a NEW HORIZON minibus to a home for the handicapped, for example, or appearing on the green stage at a cricket match. Celebrities draw the crowds, the crowds give us the money. That is how the Charity functions.

This little book is dedicated to them in gratitude for all their help in producing it, and for all their efforts in support of the Charity year in and year out. All the royalties from the sale of the book will go towards achieving our charitable objectives.

Have a good read and the odd belly laugh.

ANTHONY SWAINSON OBE
Director

Digs I Have Dug

IT seems very appropriate to me that the proceeds of a book on theatrical digs should go to charity, because, in the days when such establishments played an important part in my life, I found that one of the most important qualities needed in judging one's digs was charity. Also faith and hope. Not to mention mercy.

It also seems appropriate that they should be called 'digs'. Nobody is quite clear about the derivation of this word, but I believe we can't overlook the archaeological connection. There is an obvious link. Indeed, I understand that modern science has now evolved a system of carbon-dating the encrustations on sauce bottles to determine whether the premises were originally established in the neolithic or palaeolithic eras – although there has been no breakthrough as yet in the research to discover why some landladies fell into the pterodactyl class while others favoured the Tyrannosaurus Rex. However, this is mere historical background. Let us move on to the theatrical digs as I knew them.

I wonder if they still exist as I knew them, those lace-curtained Lubiankas, huddled in streets designed by Doctor Caligari and populated by shifty-looking dogs and cats who, if they still had their tails, were visitors – those front parlours, awash with horsehair, bamboo plant-stands, red velvet drapes bobbled along the edges, and brass light switches which, when turned on, made the room go darker – those murky passages paved with linoleum the colour and durability of wet cardboard, redolent of boot polish, bicycles, and cabbage-water, leading to the dank cavern of the scullery where crouched the master of the house, a red-eyed, gooseberry-bristled charmer, complete with muffler, cloth cap, and floor-brushing knuckles, who could have taken over the lead in 'The

Hairy Ape' without make-up and no questions asked.

Of course, there were many exceptions to this Edgar Allan Poe-land. There must have been. Theatrical colleagues (some in this very book) have told me of beautifully appointed apartments, ideally situated, some overlooking the sea, some overlooking local beauty spots, some overlooking anything as long as you paid your rent; others that sounded like the Taj Mahal with wall-to-wall hot water and unlimited use of cruet. I must have been just unlucky because what I got ranged from (while at the Majestic, Runcorn) a 'Penthouse', which turned out to be an attic so tiny that the mice were hunchbacked to a 'Studio Flat' (Corn Exchange, Shepton Mallet), a cellar so bereft of comfort that the cockroaches used to get food parcels from church mice. I did once think I'd got lucky. The advertisement read: 'Cosy yet light and airy accommodation with superior elevation. Complete security. Built-in gymnasium'. All true, I admit. But I did get awfully sick of trying to sleep on that little trapeze, running up and down that little ladder to see myself in the mirror, and being woken up to answer irrelevant questions like, 'Who's a pretty boy, then?' Furthermore, I considered it a gross imposition on my good nature to try and pass off grounsel as breakfast cereal.

And that brings us to another vexed question on this subject: the food in theatrical digs. Again, fellow-thespians have set me salivating like the Hound of the Baskervilles with stories of exotic delicacies and abundant helpings to rival Desperate Dan's cow-pie or those mounds of mashed potato studded with sausages that always appeared in the *Beano* just after the Toff says to Our Hero, 'Here, my good man – take this fiver and treat yourself to a slap-up dinner at the Hotel de Posh!' Well, all I can say is that my own gastronomic experiences in digs were somewhat different. I'm thinking here in particular of what were over-optimistically called 'after-theatre suppers'. When you returned after the second house, these awaited you on the parlour table, sometimes decently shrouded in a damp winding-sheet, as though recovered from the *Titanic*, or exposed to the pitiless glare of the 15-watt bulb.

Sometimes the supper was a simple salmonella sandwich, but more often it consisted of two slices of bread and butter curling in agony beside a dinner plate on which cowered one shrivelled lettuce leaf, one wizened tomato, one slice of ham cut as fine (and as tasty) as gossamer silk, and one drumstick looking more like a matchstick – leading in one case at least to the suspicion that it had belonged to the previous tenant of the 'light and airy accommodation' I mentioned above.

Nor can I claim that any of the other meals were much different. In fact, they all seemed designed to demonstrate the truth of the rule set out by the great Stephen Leacock in his 'Boarding-House Geometry': 'Any two meals at a boarding-house shall together be less than one square meal'.

Mind you, my experience of digs goes back a good few years. They say that distance lends enchantment to the view. So these places probably weren't nearly as splendid as I've made out.

But of course the young are resilient. I don't remember suffering all that much at the time. In fact, to tell the truth, those digs to me, as a beginner in the business, were all I could ask for. (Also, all I could afford.) They were really a second home to me. They're where I learned my trade. They made a man of me. And do you think I'd have swopped them for the bridal suite at the Ritz? Are you kidding? I'd have swopped them for a decently-built dog-kennel.

And what's more, I did. (Gaiety, Bootle.)

Caught in the Act

THE great comedian Sandy Powell used to tell the story of how, as a seventeen-year-old, he went to Scarborough to appear in a week's variety. He was – and remained throughout his life – a very decent-living chap and he was horrified, on this occasion, by the way the landlady of the theatrical boarding house pursued him amorously.

He was vastly relieved when the end of the week arrived and he was able to leave – but upon reaching the railway station, he realised that he had left his ticket at the lodgings. Apprehensively he crept back and went around to the kitchen door, thinking his return would go unnoticed. Not so. On the kitchen table was the landlady, stark naked, and poised above her, also stark naked, was the tenor from the local operatic society.

Horrified, the young Sandy Powell took in this scene. Then the landlady saw him. She blushed all over. 'Oh, Mr Powell,' she said. 'You will think I'm a flirt!'

One Night of Glamour

IN 1966 I left art school with a BA and a curious sense of unfulfilment. Having supplemented my meagre student's grant by making a fearful row in pubs with a few chums, also known as the Bonzo Dog Doo Dah Band, I happily exchanged Academia for the Glamour of Show Biz. Some twenty years on, I still haven't found any real glamour, but I suppose I came quite close to it in a cabaret club in Bolton, Lancs . . .

Throughout the closing overs of the sixties, 'Never had it so good' Britain boasted many such establishments and honest folk flocked within to wallow in the pleasures of booze, scampi in the basket, gambling, quite near the top 'names' and their 'supports'. In those days the Band would 'double'. We would play one club at around 9pm and then drive anything up to thirty miles to another, set up and perform again at 11pm. Hysteria was not uncommon. So it was one starlit, balmy night in Bolton we were shown to our dressing room. A vibrantly utilitarian area furnished with standing rolls of lino, folding tables, stacking chairs, mops and buckets, dead curtains and a job lot of assorted ashtrays, all tastefully arranged around a condemned sofa. Directly across a narrow corridor a gallant army of women were busy deep-frying and stock-piling chips as numerous as bullets for World War II. The air was thick with the scent of battle; however, we were not alone. Two other acts were to precede us in the public arena.

The first was a lively little old man with a fierce body odour problem matched only by his constant enthusiasm. He shared our dressing room and the Band gladly gave him the lion's share of the limited space. 'They're a terrific crowd out there,' he reassured us all as he lit a candle and held a cork to the flame. 'Great people,' he went on, blacking his face with the burnt cork. The audience was quite audible. They gave out a constant rumble of lager-induced excitement and bonhomie, a kind of prolonged satisfied roar. It was against this background noise the little man was duly announced. A piano tinkled bravely and a thin voice piped out a succession of Al Jolson favourites, for some twenty minutes. There was no applause and the droning continued throughout. Face streaked with perspiration and smelling even worse, the Jazz Singer returned triumphantly to the dressing room. 'Terrific bunch out there, lads, I've warmed them up for you!' We thanked him and bought him a pint.

The second act, who did not share our dressing room but were given the privacy of a large broom cupboard, was a duo of remarkably unkempt young women. We saw them in the corridor carrying their assorted props. They wore surprisingly dull silver swimsuits and were completely indifferent to the problems of bikini-line. Perched precariously on top of hastily backcombed hair, each sported a plastic rhinestone tiara. They had earrings to match. Teetering on silver high-heeled shoes, they unsteadily manoeuvred a piece of 8' x 4' soft-board through the crowd. A little curious, we decided to watch them practise their art.

They began with three Indian clubs each. The concentration required to keep them spinning in the air did not allow the girls to smile. They positioned themselves to juggle all six between them. At the first attempt, four of them collided and fell to the floor with a loud clump that caused a momentary lull in the crowd noise. After the fourth attempt they abandoned the trick.

Next, they both put on seaside cowboy hats. One took a large whip and the other put a very long piece of rolled-up newspaper in her mouth. The whip cracked and a piece of paper the size of a postage stamp flew off. Everyone suddenly paid attention. The whip cracked again. A miss. Crack. Another miss. Tension mounted, the crowd became uneasy. Presumably the intention was to remove a small piece of the newspaper each time, making it shorter and shorter. Crack went the whip again. This time the entire roll of paper was taken away cleanly at the lips. Relieved, the audience returned to their drinking and droning and we rushed tight-lipped back to the dressing room to indulge in a ten-minute bout of uncontrollable giggling.

It took that long to achieve a sufficient measure of composure to venture back into the wings. The piece of 8′ x 4′ soft-board was in place and erect. One of the girls stood spread-eagled in front of it. The other tottered about, clashing a bunch of knives against each other. Both girls looked as though they were hooked on Valium. The plucky trio stopped playing 'The Magnificent Seven' and the drummer played a roll on the snare. The audience gaped in horror. A knife was held aloft and flung, rapidly followed by all the others. Of the dozen or so knives only two stuck in. One on the edge of the board, only just, dangling limply by its tip, and the other firmly embedded perilously near the girl's throat. The thunderous applause lasted long enough for them both to nonchalantly pick up the knives and take a bow.

At last it was our turn. Light-headed after so much excitement, I took with me one of the many large ashtrays from the dressing room and a new tin of smoke powder. In those days we began the act with 'Rule Britannia' ending with an explosion on 'slaves'. A cheap trick to get the audience's attention. However, this evening I played the piano with one hand and emptied the entire contents of the tin of smoke powder into the large ashtray with the other, and lit it. By the time we got to the explosion the entire club was thick with dense smoke. Everyone, Band included, left the club and stood in the street, clutching pints and droning for fifteen minutes until the smoke cleared. Casually the audience returned to their tables and scampi in the basket, and we returned to the stage. It was a great evening with a terrific crowd. Everybody had a good time.

Billy's Greatest Performance

WAY back in the early fifties I was booked for eight weeks as a support act, to appear in a variety show with Ralph Slater, the hypnotist, topping the bill.

For us variety performers it was a very difficult show to work in because the type of people he attracted were not the usual family audiences, that is to say, the regulars that religiously went week after week. He attracted people from all walks of life who came out of sheer curiosity to see what marvels he could perform.

Touring in variety on your own can be a very lonely life, so I chummed up with the lead of a comedy mime act, Billy. He was an old pro, had been in the business for years, knew all the ropes, and had a marvellous address book of digs. He took charge of all our accommodation, and his choice was excellent.

On the Saturday night we all travelled up to Leeds ready to open on the Monday at the Empire.

When we boarded the train we discovered we were sharing a sleeping compartment with Ralph Slater's valet. He was a nice little chap, and surprised us with his lovely sense of humour.

It must have been the early hours of the morning when the door of our compartment crashed open, the lights came on and framed in the doorway was a guard from first class. He said, 'Which one of you is Ralph Slater's valet?' The voice underneath me said, 'I am.' The guard said, 'Well follow me, he wants you in a hurry.' The valet left, still struggling into his trousers. A few minutes later he came back laughing his head off, and as he was opening his valise he said, 'You're never going to believe this . . . a bleedin' hypnotist and he wants his sleeping pills.'

Unfortunately for us, Leeds had a couple of long-running shows on and all Billy's favourite digs had been taken, so he was forced to choose an address from Equity's book of Theatrical Accommodation. I asked him if he knew them. He said, 'No, your guess is as good as mine.'

It was about 10am when we finally found our digs on this cold bleak rainy Sunday morning. We stood in the porch and instead of Billy knocking at the door he started searching the walls. I said, 'What the hell are you looking for?' He said, 'Any signs of warning left by other pros who've stayed here in the past, such as NBG – no bloody good – or KITP – kipper in the piano.' As he knocked on the door he said, 'I didn't find anything so we could be lucky.'

As soon as the door opened I didn't like the look of things. A tall thin woman stood there in a black dress, wiping her hands on her apron. She had a hatchet-type face with her hair pulled back in a bun at the back of her neck. She said, 'What do you two want at this time in the morning?' Billy said, 'We're at the Empire next week and I booked two single rooms for myself and Mr Varney here.' She said, 'You might have booked two single rooms, but all I can let you have is one room with two single beds. Do you want to take it or not?' There was nothing we could do but accept. We picked up our cases and were about to enter when she said, 'Oh no you don't, I wasn't expecting you until this evening, so come back at five o'clock.' As an afterthought she said, 'Oh alright' – we fully expected her to say you can come in, instead she carried on: 'You can leave your cases in the passage, but don't leave them so as people can fall over them.'

Apart from spending a couple of hours in a pub at lunchtime over a sandwich and a beer, the rest of the time we spent miserably mooching the cold wet streets of Leeds, bemoaning our luck.

It seemed an eternity before five o'clock arrived and we were back knocking at the door. The door opened and without a word of greeting she said, 'Your bedroom's on the second floor, first on the right.' As we lugged our cases up the two flights, I wondered where she kept her broomstick.

The room had no carpet on the floor, just the bare lino. There were two single beds with a chair either side, and a rickety old wardrobe. And it was freezing.

After we'd had a wash in the toilet cum bathroom, we changed into dry clothes and came downstairs. The fire roaring up the chimney in the lounge looked very inviting. We were about to sit in the armchairs either side of the fire when the battleaxe dashed in saying, 'You don't eat in here, this is the students' room. I've laid your table up in the little room next door.' The little room next door was a replica of the bedroom except this had a table and two chairs. She pointed to the table saying, 'I've made you a cold meat salad,' then walked out.

As we sat down to eat Billy said, 'This is all we need in a freezing cold room like this, a bleedin' cold salad.'

The meal was dreadful – the lettuce was completely relaxed and had dozed off, and the few slices of cucumber lay there as if they'd given up all hope of being eaten. Although we made an attempt to eat it, as hungry as we were, we couldn't. Finally Billy pushed his plate aside saying, 'This is disgusting. If things don't improve by tomorrow night I'm going to do something about it.' I said, 'Such as?' He said, 'You wait and see.'

Monday's meals were as bad as the salad, and when on Tuesday morning there was no sign of an egg, or a rasher, just cornflakes and cold toast, Billy said, 'Right, that's it . . . I'm not standing any more of this,' and got straight up and went out.

I sat there without a clue as to what he had in mind, when suddenly I heard him say, in a very Actor Laddie voice: 'Can I have a word with you in here, madam?'

As they entered the room she was saying, 'Well, what's this all about?' Billy pulled himself up to his full height of five foot five and said: 'It's my duty, madam, to inform you that I am an Inspector for Equity looking into complaints made by members of my profession about this establishment. Your address is in the Equity book. We do not expect to be treated like royalty, but we do ask to be treated like human beings.

Your accommodation and food are a disgrace, to say nothing about your disgusting behaviour towards us. It is only fair to inform you that I shall be reporting to the Committee today confirming that past complaints about your establishment have been justified. We shall be back for our luggage at 12.30. Come on, Reg.' And before she had time to open her mouth, we were closing the street door.

When we got outside I collapsed, tears were rolling down my cheeks. I said, 'That was a great act, mate, but what a load of old cobblers.' He said, 'Maybe, but it might do some good.'

It was obvious she had been awaiting our return from the theatre because immediately she opened the door she ushered us towards our little dining room.

When we went in I thought we were in the wrong house – it was like Cinderella's transformation scene. There was a beautiful fire going, with two easy chairs, one either side of the fireplace, a very nice rug covering the lino and pretty chintz curtains draping the window. The table had a white lace tablecloth on it, laid with her best cutlery and plates.

She ignored the transformation of the room and just went on to say how sorry she was. Yes, she did owe us an apology, it was due to the government insisting on her taking in students, twelve in all. The excuses went on and on. Eventually Billy cut in to stop her rabbitting on and seeing that things had greatly improved, he told her – calling her darling now, not madam – that he was unable to get through to the office and seeing that she had made this great effort to make us more comfortable, there was no need for her to worry, as he would not now be doing so.

Needless to say, for the rest of the week we lived like fighting cocks and once, whilst enjoying one of our 'cordon bleu' meals I said to Billy, 'Did you know this would happen?' He said, 'There was a strong possibility it would – well it did the last time I did this act!'

Loo Training

THIS story was told to me by my mother. She had been sharing digs in Blackpool in the same house as Rob Wilton, the popular comedian.

The toilet was at the end of a long corridor illuminated by a bare bulb. It was a primitive affair and you really had to be in need to make the effort to go there.

One night, Rob Wilton came back to his digs more than a little merry at one o'clock in the morning. He ambled down the corridor, responded to the call of nature, and then he tried to pull the ancient chain. Nothing happened. He tried again and again but it wouldn't work. Finally he gave up the idea and turned to leave.

At the far end of the corridor, awakened by the commotion, the formidable landlady stood in her voluminous candlewick gown, hair in curlers, arms crossed.

'You'll never get it to work that way, Mr Wilton,' she declared. 'You've got to walk away from it and then suddenly turn round and surprise it!'

Going Going

IN 1966 I was playing the lead in *Boeing Boeing* at the Duchess Theatre in London. I had been appearing in the play for many months, but one is never quite prepared for those embarrassing situations that can unexpectedly occur. The character that I played, Robert, is up from the country visiting an old friend, who has organised his private life in a most sophisticated way. He has a wonderful arrangement with three air hostesses, and has so planned everything that as one flies out the other flies in. Something is bound to go wrong with such an ingenious plan, which is of course the basis of the play, and this begins to happen when Robert is in the flat alone.

The unexpected situation that caused such embarrassment occurred at the beginning of Act Two. The maid had gone to buy some cigarettes for the German air hostess, who had returned without warning, met Robert, and a mutual attraction has resulted. The girl excuses herself and goes into the bedroom, leaving Robert alone on the stage. At this moment the maid enters with the cigarettes. Robert immediately has the idea to take the cigarettes, so that he can give them to the girl personally. He asks the maid to hand them over, but she refuses, so Robert grabs the packet from her hand, and then dismisses her to the kitchen.

That is what should have happened. On this particular occasion, I grabbed the cigarettes out of her hand as usual with a flourish. Unfortunately I could not have held the packet properly, because it flew out of my hand, over the footlights and into the orchestra pit, which contained a single piano. My mind raced. For practical reasons concerned with the plot, we could not continue the play without the cigarettes. I thought of suggesting that the maid went and bought another packet, but quickly realised that that would be impossible as she had already established it had taken her a long time to buy the first one. Also, what would I do in the meantime while she was off the stage?

I glanced into the orchestra pit and saw the cigarettes lying beside the piano. In a situation like this it is always helpful if you've worked as a solo artist. I looked over the footlights to see where the cigarettes lay. I looked puzzled, and then looked at the audience conveying my dilemma. They started to laugh, which gave me confidence. The agonised look on the face of the maid added to the situation. Realising the audience understood the dilemma that I was in, without appreciating the fact that we could not continue the play without the cigarettes, I thought of a scheme.

We had established on my first entrance in the opening scene that there was a huge picture-window in my friend's flat which was over the footlights, so I began ad-libbing, still trying to think of a way out of this difficult situation. I said: 'It's a pity that the window was open.' This received a big laugh – I was keeping the audience with me. I then pretended to look out of the window – in other words, over the footlights – and saw that I could climb out into the orchestra pit by stepping down on to the piano. I continued ad-libbing: 'Oh look, the cigarettes have landed on the window ledge of the flat below.' I proceeded to climb over the footlights and into the orchestra pit, lowering myself down by holding onto the edge of the stage until my feet touched the piano. The audience were not only very amused by this, but they actually applauded, which I felt was not so much complimenting me on my inventiveness or agility, but reassuring me they appreciated the difficulty. I have always found that, provided the audience knows what is going on, they are always sympathetic and thoroughly enjoy the artist's efforts to cover the unfortunate mistake. This is certainly true in a comedy, and of course it is much easier in a comedy to ad-lib your way out of an unexpected or difficult situation.

I managed to climb onto the piano without doing myself an injury, jumped to the floor of the orchestra pit – now unseen by the audience – picked up the cigarettes, and then climbed back the way I had descended. At the same time I had to keep ad-libbing in order not to lose the audience's attention, so I kept a running commentary about the neighbours who lived in the flat below. I have forgotten the exact words, but it was along the lines of: 'They landed on their window-box . . . their geraniums look very pretty . . . I'm glad they weren't in, otherwise they might have thought I was a burglar . . . I certainly don't look like the window cleaner . . . I'm glad I didn't slip, it's a big drop to the ground floor from this flat . . .'

This dialogue covered the climbing in and out of the 'apparent' window. My final ad-lib to the actress who was playing the maid, who had remained somewhat paralysed and certainly nonplussed on stage throughout, was: 'I hope in future you make sure that window is kept shut!' This line not only amused the audience, but absolutely 'corpsed' her. She doubled up with laughter – it was probably a release of tension, knowing that everything was now all right. I told her not to laugh at my misfortune, and suggested that she went back to the kitchen.

The play continued as normal – and as written! I hope I never have such an unnerving, or potentially dangerous, situation to cope with again.

Acting Down-Wind

ONE problem that faces anyone who is asked to contribute a story or two on the subject of theatrical digs is that of dating yourself. They don't exist any more. To admit to having experienced them is to accept that it is pointless having your agent suggest you for Romeo next week. This is a pity because at last I understand Romeo.

Today's young actors, jetting between exotic dates in Billingham and Rhyl (out of season) on salaries of £110 or more, stay in hotels. The 'stars' might even have a shower *en suite!* Not for them the problem of deciding just when to have your one permitted bath per week. Sunday was always a good day. You could afford to luxuriate, let the strain (of doubling the soldier in the first act with the Kentish villager in the third) ease with pleasurable pain from a weary body. The only problem was that by Thursday nobody would act down-wind of you. It only needed three members of the cast to adopt the same policy and it played havoc with the director's carefully orchestrated production. I had excellent digs in Belfast. Four pounds a week, but I was earning ten. This included the usual weekly bath and one shilling for every extra one. The problem of extra baths didn't arise. The most hazardous thing about Belfast in those days was an actor called Jimmy Ellis. I used to meet him in McGlade's most mornings, have a Guinness and then set off on the daily search for his bike which he had lost the day before. By about the fourth bar we'd have found it. By the seventh or eighth we'd have lost it again. And next day we'd start again. This was great fun, but although Guinness was very cheap, there weren't many shillings left over for extra baths.

There was another member of the company in my digs. A beautiful red-haired girl whom I hated. She used to have a bath every morning (her parents were either terribly wealthy or she didn't like Guinness), and would always take it at exactly the time I wanted to use the bathroom. This meant I was faced with the decision as to whether to miss breakfast (difficult, as I was probably meeting Jimmy at ten-thirty) or wait until I got to the theatre before I parted company with yesterday's Guinness (virtually impossible). But her worst sin was that she suspected that I lusted after her little (clean) body, and she wouldn't let me have it. I got my own back. One night she contrived to go on stage in the part of the beautiful heroine with one false eyelash glued on upside down. This gave her a ghastly, squint-eyed leer. I didn't tell her. Every actor, every night, everywhere hopes that somebody 'from London' is out front. I hope somebody from London was out front that night.

Landladies have long memories. They will regale you for hours with stories of the eminent people who have slept in your bed. I had a whole week of Ivor Emmanual in Cardiff. He'd stayed in those same digs five years previously. Landladies' daughters have even longer memories. On my very first job — twice nightly with the Penguin Players — I could only afford bed and breakfast, so I came to a very pleasant arrangement with the landlady's daughter, who used to sneak a late-night snack up to my room to keep my strength up, so to speak. I had to give the theatre my notice eventually as, ironically, it was not my waistline that was expanding, but hers. Eight years later I was doing one of those successful television series and she tracked me down to remind me of the promises I had made over a luke warm lasagne. She must have had a sense of humour, however, because she invited me out for a meal that evening.

Of course, it goes without saying that all landladies run 'good' houses. To make quite certain that nothing happens to mar anyone's reputation, they never sleep. Just try taking that little girl who's playing the innocent shepherdess in Act Two back to your room to run over her lines, and no matter what the time of day, there's the landlady on the stairs to suggest that there's nothing that can be done in your room that can't be done in the parlour. She's right, of course, but her company can inhibit your performance. I was in digs in Swansea when true love broke out between the leading man and his beautiful co-star. For a blissful week he found himself sharing her bed. At the end of the week she was charged double for the room. This, the landlady explained, was because two people had been using it. Heaven knows how she knew. The leading man protested that, despite the unscheduled romance, he had paid for his own room anyway. Ah, said the landlady, but had she known that his room was going to be unused she could have let it to somebody else. She had lost money on the arrangement. Very thrifty, the Welsh.

But perhaps the best story actually happened to a friend of a friend of mine – as all the best stories invariably do! He was playing Nottingham and all the digs on the Equity list were full. It was the time of Goosey Fair and the town was bursting at the seams with hustlers, hookers and fakers. At last he found a room in a very convivial house full of circus folk. He has always maintained that he had one of the happiest weeks of his life with these cosmopolitan, exotic people. They were at the opposite end of the great entertainment spectrum to his own, and just as anxious to hear his stories of theatrical triumphs as he was to hear tales of derring-do in foreign lands. Many a crate of brown ale was drunk to see them into the small hours.

His only problem was the one of sleep. Not only was he not getting to bed until late, but once there he was always woken from drunken slumber by a strange thump, thump, thumping which seemed to come from nearby, but had no explanation. He mentioned this the next day to his circus friends, but they had heard nothing. By the third night he was becoming quite neurotic because of the phantom thumping. It was not so much the regularity of it, but the fact that there was no apparent reason for it and nobody else seemed to be aware of it. On the fourth night he was in deep sleep following another night of carousing and unlikely stories, when he was woken once again by the same thump, thump, thump. He lay for a moment, almost distracted by his need to solve the mystery, when he became aware of another need, brought about by the brown ale. He left his room and padded down the corridor, and there he saw, framed in the open bathroom door, one of the midgets with the circus, obviously having just answered the same needs as those besetting my friend, and jumping desperately to reach the chain – *thump, thump, thump*.

Ideas Above My Station

I was picked up at the train station by my landlady. She was about seventy years old and bright as a button. She drove a large beaten-up Volvo Estate, into which I loaded three suitcases and a box. I had arrived in Exeter for my very first job, six months at the Northcott Theatre. I had also brought with me my motorbike. She climbed into her car, I onto my bike and off we went through a town I had never seen before. Within minutes I had completely lost all sense of direction and was feeling more than a little homesick.

Eventually we stopped in a small back street in an even smaller housing estate, somewhere on the outskirts of town. She was very spritely for seventy and no sooner had we stopped than she was out of her car and unloading my luggage. I was still trying to work out which of these singularly unattractive rabbit hutches was going to be my new home.

'Don't worry, dear, it's not one of these.' My anxiety must have been written all over my face. 'Our's is a nice house. It's up there on the hill.'

I looked to where she was pointing and saw a small white gate cut into a huge privet hedge.

'The drive is far too narrow to take cars I'm afraid, so we'll have to walk. It's not very far.'

What she hadn't told me was that the house was at the very top of the hill or that the hill was very steep, running right through the middle of a wood, or that it would take us about half an hour to do the walk, and it was beginning to get dark.

We finally made it to the top, tired, breathless and with rather a lot of my luggage left at strategic points all the way up.

'You can collect it later, dear, once you've got your breath back.'

However now the ground levelled out and the trees gave

way to lawns, leading at their end to the welcome sight of my first theatrical digs. I had organised it from London. The Theatre had sent me a list of possibilities and having telephoned a few, I had chosen this one. Firstly because of the cost – £16 a week – and secondly because I had been told that it was a little bit different.

The latter turned out to be the understatement of the century, though from the outside the house looked nothing out of the ordinary at all. Except for the fact that it appeared to have twelve front doors, spaced evenly all the way along the face of the house.

'Won't you step this way, dear, and I'll show you around.'

She took me to the back where some steps led down to a small basement entrance. The door opened onto a vast old-fashioned kitchen complete with two huge cast-iron Agas.

'This is the kitchen,' she said. 'You can cook in here if you like and eat in here as well, it's all pretty straightforward.'

From there we looked around the rest of the ground floor which consisted of an equally large sitting room and a very small hallway, dominated completely by a wonderful spiral staircase. 'It came from the back of an old trolley bus,' I was told. 'Come along now and I'll show you your room.'

We climbed the stairs, my landlady allowing me to go first; she knew the surprise that was waiting for me at the top. The entire upper level of the house was made from two matching railway carriages with a covered corridor between them. Without saying a word, my landlady passed me and walked down the length of the passageway, leaving me open-mouthed at the top of the stairs. She finally stopped at the last door of the right-hand carriage. 'You've got the guard's van, I'm afraid, but don't worry, it's very comfortable.'

She was absolutely right, it was very comfortable and quite the most remarkable room I have ever stepped into. Everything in it was original, except for the bed of course, right down to the small windows allowing the guard to see the rest of the train without putting his head outside. The loo, down the hall, was a converted second-class compartment, as was the bathroom opposite. The other two bedrooms were also conversions; they used to be first-class compartments and still had their washstands and fold-down beds to prove it.

I looked around everything and then asked if perhaps we could have a cup of tea. I wanted to hear the story of how all this had arrived on the top of a hill in Exeter.

It turned out that some years ago she had met and fallen in love with a man who called himself 'The Captain'; they had wanted to get married but neither of them had been able to get a divorce. However they both loved trains, and having seen two carriages for sale, decided to buy them, build themselves a dream home and live together in blissful sin. During their work, however, they had sadly run out of money and had been forced instead to rent out the rooms and live in a caravan in the garden until the job was finished.

'There's a banker in one room at the moment and the secretary of the British Hang Gliding Team in the other. He likes to go onto the top of Dartmoor and jump off,' she told me secretively.

I asked her when she and the Captain were thinking of moving back in; after all the house looked pretty finished to me.

'Oh no, dear, we're not going to do that,' she said. 'We could have moved back in ages ago but we've rather got used to the caravan now. Besides it means that the house is always full of people and we like to have people about, after all that's what the trains were built for in the first place, wasn't it.'

I stayed there for a few weeks before finally getting a flat of my own. I can't remember the address but often wonder if it's still there, and if my friend and her Captain still own the train on the hill.

Hot Seat

I once stayed in digs in Bradford that only afforded outside toilets. As the houses were in one long terrace, so were the loos, stretching across the bottoms (how apt!) of the tiny back gardens. The landlady had a thing about electric light. It must not be used after eleven o'clock. Consequently, in case you wished to go to the loo after that, she provided a torch, a back door key, and instructions as to how to avoid the coal bunker in the dark.

One night I was taken short after midnight, and grabbing my torch and key, I made my uncertain way towards the row of outside toilets. Approaching what I thought was the loo door that corresponded with the digs, I was startled by the rattle of a casement window being flung open. Out popped the becurlered head of my landlady who screamed out, 'Mr Crowther! Are you going to the lavatory?'

'Yes,' I whispered furtively.

She said: 'Well don't go in that one, luv. It's next door's and we're not speaking!'

No Solids

Unfortunately the good old (and not so good old) theatrical digs are things of the past. They are, however, remembered with affection by most old pros. My first experience of syrups (I leave the reader to work out the rhyming slang) was way back in 1927. I never actually came across those with the convenience at the bottom of the garden but I have known plenty who have.

My old friend Clifford Mollison (how we miss him) once told me he visited one such and pulled the chain (actually a piece of rope) several times without result. Eventually he gave it a hell of a tug while looking down for the flush, and a great dollop of sand hit him on the back of the neck.

Doris Hare told me she once went into the kitchen to ask if it would be all right to go out to the back, whereupon the landlady opened the back door and shouted, 'Dad! Come off and let the lady come on.'

One lady had a downstairs loo which was strictly private and out of bounds to lodgers. One day an actor got desperate and had to dash in – but was spotted. 'What are you doing in there?' said the landlady. 'I'll give you two guesses,' was the reply. After a pause she said, 'Well, no solids.'

Digs experiences are not all lavatory humour. The visitors' books always contained some interesting items. 'Shall always be pleased to return and recommend. Try Ma's black pudding.' Landladies were invariably addressed as 'Ma'. Another entry was 'Found Mrs . . . a very comfortable woman.' And there was the very proud one who said 'Look what nice Mr George Robey put in my book: "Quoth the Raven".'

Perhaps my favourite digs incident is the one which backfired on Bobby Howes. He and his friends had a bottle of sherry which kept disappearing until it was nearly empty.

Evidently the landlady was helping herself. So they did the unpardonable thing. When the bottle was empty, they urinated into it. It still kept disappearing. At the end of the week the landlady hoped they would return. 'No, not after what happened to our sherry,' said Bobby. 'Oh that,' said the landlady. 'I've been putting it into your soup.'

'Em's as Dies Will be the Lucky Ones

Very well, then. They say confession is good for the soul. It was some years ago, m'lud, at the Old Mermaid Theatre (by 'Old' I mean under the benign rule of Sir Bernard Miles, as he then was). I was giving, not for the first time, Squire Trelawney in *Treasure Island*, only this time it was the musical version. All I can say in mitigation, m'lud, is that as an actor I am strangely disciplined, and not given to excess, unless there is, as on this occasion, a sudden explosion in the head, and then, I'm afraid, there can be disaster of Krakatoa-like proportions.

Perhaps I should describe the sequence of events as they occurred twice nightly without incident for several weeks previously, which is in itself something of a miracle. It was near the beginning of the piece at the 'Admiral Benbow', a public house owned, you may remember, by young Jim Hawkins' mother. Blind Pew and a number of pirates have arrived to wrest the map of Treasure Island from an old 'sea-captain', who as a result of over-exertion in its defence, has a heart attack. The Seventh Cavalry arrive, the Squire, Dr Livesey and several others, and Blind Pew is run over, off stage, by a pair of coconut shells. The pirates disperse. The Doctor and I are shown the map by young Jim, and I suggest that we obtain a boat and set off at once. There immediately followed the single most ludicrous cue for song in the history of the musical. Dr Livesey suggests that I keep quiet about the map and the voyage, walls have ears, etc, and I reply angrily: 'Dr Livesey! My lips are sealed!' – Note from orchestra, and I launch into song—

'There's a place called Treasure Island
Men would long to see . . .' (or something)

Now as if singing this song was not sufficient (and if Equity was half the union it should be, in my view there would be a statutory lying-down period of at least five minutes for anyone who has just sung a song, out loud, on a stage), as we hit the final note, the lights went out, and I would set off to the rear of the stage in pitch darkness, tearing off my topcoat, waistcoat and hat, to meet somewhere in the stygian gloom a wardrobe mistress, holding infinitely more elaborate and weightier versions of the same for a quick-change into Trelawney the Admiral. I then had to grope about for a ladder, scale this, and erupt, breathing heavily, on to a rostrum some ten feet above stage-level, and then, still, to all intents and purposes, blind as the late Pew, pick my way through various barrels and maritime properties to the front, where the Doctor (Eric Flynn) and Jim Hawkins (a scholarly little fellow whose name escapes me) waited for me. As I joined them, up came the lights, and we were discovered on the dock at Bristol with me, the Squire, embarking on several paragraphs about chartering the *Hispaniola*, finding a Captain, and a crew, and, luckiest find of all, a sea-cook of undoubted experience. 'His name', I would declaim in ringing tones, 'is Long John Silver, and he lost a leg in the service of this Country!' Whether or not this was in some appalling culinary mishap in the Roaring Forties, or a sacrificial gesture to vary the crew's usual diet of hard tack, was not mentioned, but after a few more exchanges to establish that Young Jim would be joining us, down went the lights on us, and up they came centre-stage to reveal a large chorus of pirates in Long John's Bristol hostelry, who would burst into a rousing nautical drinking number.

Well, as I say, this all went pretty smoothly, m'lud, up to the night in question. I put it all down to exhaustion; I was larger in those days and singing and quick-changes and ladder groping take their toll. The song went quite well. I made my rendezvous with the wardrobe mistress and exchanged garments in a reasonable time. I had the usual trouble on the ladder – the heaviness of the coat, the smallness of the trap through which I had to work the enormous hat – but there I

was at altitude, finally beside my colleagues, and as the lights
came up I spouted: 'There she stands, Doctor, the *Hispaniola* –
300 tons [or whatever] of weathered teak'. The audience hung,
as I like to think is customary, upon my every word. There was
no warning of the looming Vesuvius. The pirates assembled
below in the dark unaware that they were entering a wine bar
in Pompeii.

'His name,' I said, having reached the bit about the cook
(Parrot in a Basket the Speciality of the House), 'is Long John
Silver and . . .' (BOOM!) I can't remember what I say next. All
the grey cells had vanished in the blast. The mind was empty. I
stood like a zombie in Tesco's, peering blankly at the shelves.
They weren't shelves, of course, they were rows of seats, full of
parents and children, shifting uncomfortably. I turned my
attention to young Jim, mainly because his face had turned
bright red and he was making noises like a boiling kettle. The
Doctor (Eric Flynn) was laughing quite openly. The entire play
had ground to a stop.

Unknown to me, Sir Bernard Miles, Long John Silver to the
manner born, in full costume, parrot included, but with both
legs on as he had not yet hitched up the missing one, had
stepped into a pool of light beneath us, in full view of all, and
was shouting in a stage whisper, 'He lost a leg! He lost a leg!'

This may have inspired the Doctor, for inspired he surely
was. He stopped laughing, laid a steadying hand upon my
shoulder and provided me with possibly the finest prompt ever
offered by one actor to another. In his best bedside manner, he
enquired: 'This Long John Silver, how many legs has he got?'

Like manna from Heaven, which I always imagined was
porridge-like, the grey cells, which are becoming increasingly
porridge-like, began to pour back in. Verbose to the last and
groping again, but this time in the bright light, I replied: 'A
fascinating question, Doctor, and you as a medical man will be
more than interested to learn that he has but the one. He lost
the other. Somewhere. Or other.'

Despite the fact that young Jim never got another word out,
though his colour improved, we made it to the end of our little

scene, and as the lights went down, prepared to run like hell. Possibly to Istanbul. What stopped us in our tracks, however, was the sound from below, not a roaring chorus of boozy pirates, but sounds of flatulence and sniggering. We looked down on a singular sight. Twenty desperate-looking buccaneers, mouths tightly clenched, eyes bulging against the hoots of laughter that gurgled within, silently waving their tankards to the rhythms of the orchestra. Sir Bernard could be seen in the wings, angrily tapping the one foot on view.

Eric looked at me. 'More corpses,' he said, 'than the grand finale of *Hamlet*.'

I looked at Eric. 'Istanbul?' I said, and then we ran like hell.

When The Lights Go Out

IT took us a long time to find out how she knew! The digs were in Leicester and on a tour of an ice show with close on a hundred in the cast, and all of us young, vibrant and fruity, it will come as no surprise that a considerable amount of corridor creeping went on at night. And, unless you were unlucky to bump into a fellow artist or artiste also on the creep, NO ONE KNEW OR EVEN GUESSED! So we thought . . . until breakfast next morning, when our ever cheerful landlady would push in the trolley laden with eggs and bacon, and with a broad smile and a nudge nudge, wink wink voice, announce 'Well, you two had a nice time last night and no mistake.'

'You two' having seated themselves at opposite ends of the breakfast table so as to allay any suspicion of a liaison would colour noticeably, while the rest of the cast sniggered. Sniggers that were brought to an abrupt halt with our landlady's follow up . . . 'And so did you two and you two!'

It took me a fortnight to crack how it was she could keep tabs on all of us during the operational hours of midnight and 2 am. I happened to be in her kitchen one night collecting a cup of cocoa when on the old butler's bell-board above the door a red disc dropped . . . coinciding with a room light upstairs reflecting in the glass of the greenhouse. I watched fascinated as the light was switched off and the butler's call-board cleared.

The crafty old witch had had the lights throughout the house wired into what had once been the kitchen call system, in the days when butlers, maids and footmen were around to answer milord or milady's summons. All she had to do was sit there sipping her midnight brew and she had tabs on exactly which lights were being switched on and off. From there it wasn't difficult to deduce who had moved out of *his* room and into *hers* . . . the couple unwittingly setting themselves up for the 'you two had a nice time last night' sally at breakfast.

A council of war was called amongst we nocturnal wanderers – cards on the table, how could we defeat the old faggot? No problem – down to the ironmongers and a bundle of candles. At midnight, all lights in the house registered 'switched off' on the butler's board . . . and the old crow had to wait and wait in vain.

Admittedly the neighbours across the road were convinced the house was haunted, with the sight of the creeping candles. And it wasn't until our last night there that I blew our cover by accidentally setting fire to the leading lady's bedspread. But that's another story.

The Cambridge

WHENEVER members of the wrestling profession were working in the Manchester area we always stayed at The Cambridge, a boarding house in the Old Trafford part of town. It was a real home from home, where you could come in late and always get yourself something to eat and drink and generally treat it like your own house. It was owned and run by a couple named Anna and Ernie. Anna was a large happy and warm person, who in her younger days worked the clubs in Manchester. Ernie was in his fifties, a tall thin man and by profession or occupation a 'pickpocket'. He used to work the races, county fairs, agricultural shows etc, up and down the country. It was generally accepted that he was good at his trade and the fact that he bought The Cambridge from his ill-gotten gains was evidence of this.

I arrived late one Monday night after wrestling in Oldham and found The Cambridge full; it was my own fault as I should have booked in earlier. Anna suggested that if I would share a room with a friend of Ernie's named Cyril, who would be leaving in the morning, I could have the room for the rest of the week. I had no desire to start looking for hotel rooms at that time of night, so I said it would be alright.

After some sandwiches and coffee I went up to the room. Cyril was already tucked up in his bed and fast asleep. My eyes wandered to the foot of his bed, and there propped up against it was an artificial leg. It startled me for a minute as there are not too many hotel rooms with false legs scattered around; but I soon recovered, got into bed and fell asleep.

Suddenly I was awakened by a dull thumping at regular two or three second intervals. I switched on the bedside lamp and saw that Cyril's bed was empty, though the 'leg' was still there. The truth then dawned on me. Cyril had got up to spend a penny, and not bothering to strap on his leg, had hopped along the corridor to the bathroom and back again. Whether Cyril had drunk a few pints of beer that evening or had a weak bladder I do not know, but the operation was repeated a couple of hours later.

It was 9am when I awoke and Cyril was gone, and so was the leg. I slipped on my dressing-gown and went downstairs for a cup of tea. Anna asked if I had heard Cyril during the night; I said yes and maybe the whole of Old Trafford had as well. She told me that Cyril and Ernie had gone to work the races at York. Now I could imagine Ernie doing some pocket picking as he was agile and nippy, but Cyril with his leg would be far less mobile. Anna explained the situation. Ernie did the actual stealing and would pass the wallets, money etc to Cyril who lurked nearby, so that if Ernie was challenged he would not have any evidence found on his person. Cyril used to stow the 'goodies' in his false leg. Ernie had various accomplices for this job, varying from dolly birds to middle-aged county types, and even a parson complete with 'dog collar'. I used to warn my friends that if ever they went racing to be on the lookout for a man with a false leg because it could well be Cyril, and Ernie would not be far away.

Anna and Ernie have long since passed away, and The Cambridge was pulled down to make way for a new housing development. I will always remember them with happy memories – and of course Cyril doing his Long John Silver act at the dead of night.

Mrs Simmonds' Lemon Pudding

THEATRICAL digs are now few and far between, but for years they were an institution and all actors have had their experiences – good and bad: each actor kept his own jealously guarded list and it was advisable to write well in advance to secure good accommodation.

On Sunday morning actors and scenery would meet at the railway station ready to set off for the next 'date', which invariably involved changing trains at Crewe and it was here, on windswept platforms, that we had many joyful reunions with other companies as our journeys intersected. Arriving in the new city, we found the way to our digs, to be greeted by a landlady, friendly or otherwise. (I was once shown up to my room and told, 'Remember, dear, this is your home while you're in Bournemouth – and mind – no messing up the sheets!') These landladies specialised in 'theatricals' and at their best provided better food and more comfort than most first-class hotels – and they were by no means expensive: An old actor, Edward Petley, told me in 1945 that he had never paid more than thirty shillings a week for full board. Meals were arranged to suit the peculiar hours lived by actors – breakfast at 10.30am, lunch at 2pm and supper after the performance whatever time the curtain fell. Over almost every dining room fireplace I seem to recall a reproduction of Landseer's *Monarch of the Glen* and every landlady kept her Visitors' Book filled with strange and exotic comments. Many of these stalwart ladies handed on the business to their daughters or daughters-in-law and with it went the Visitors' Book, which by then had acquired antiquarian interest.

When with two other actors I first stayed with Mrs Simmonds in Newcastle she proudly showed us her large

leatherbound book as we arrived. Dutifully we thumbed through it: the first entry was for 1886 and Frank Tyars of Henry Irving's company had written, 'You must try Mrs Simmonds' Lemon Pudding'; some time later a member of Tree's company had entered, 'Mrs Simmonds' Lemon Pudding is amazing'; later a Bensonian actor had implored, 'Don't leave without trying Mrs Simmonds' Lemon Pudding'; from Fred Terry's company, 'Mrs Simmonds' Lemon Pudding is a masterpiece'; every few months an entry asked, 'Have you sampled Mrs Simmonds' Lemon Pudding?' Thus when Mrs Simmonds (the daughter-in-law of the original Mrs Simmonds) re-entered the room we asked if we might partake of her renowned speciality: her face glowed with pride and she cooed, 'I hoped you would ask – Thursday evening.' We could hardly wait. On Thursday we raced back from the theatre and guzzled our way through the main course, the plates were removed and shortly Mrs S. came back carrying a large dish in the attitude of a portly eighteenth-century chef bearing a flaming Christmas pudding to the assembled guests in a timbered inn. She placed it in the centre of the table. On the dish was an inverted white pudding basin which she removed with a theatrical flourish, held it aloft and with 'I *know* you'll enjoy it' she left us alone. Facing us was a pure white mound of wet, sticky suet. Disenchanted, someone took a knife and, sticking it in, struck something solid . . . he cut around it and disclosed a whole lemon – skin and all. We could not disappoint her so we ate what we could of the suet on which we poured sugar and lemon juice.

Obviously, when a young housekeeper, the first Mrs Simmonds had been asked to prepare a Lemon Pudding – she had used her imagination to the apparent approval of her guests and had imparted her recipe to her daughter-in-law. When we left on the following Sunday we could write only one thing: 'Whatever you do, you must try Mrs Simmonds' Lemon Pudding!'

from *A Touch of the Memoirs*

War and Peace

I had a uniformed if not a uniform training in theatrical digs. Towards the end of the war I had exchanged the pips on the shoulder for an ENSA flash and I was wearing a rather lighter shade of khaki. We were playing an English comedy adapted from the French by a Welshman (*The Late Christopher Bean* by Emlyn Williams) and later to be performed in Rome to an unsmiling audience of Gurkhas, but somewhere south of Naples we were billeted in Army accommodation and fed by Italian cooks on NAAFI rations. We suggested that if we provided the ingredients they might like to make us a zabaglione. *Si, con piacere.* And, *con piacere*, it was served. Next morning. Cold. For breakfast.

Later during the same tour, near Ancona, we were puzzled by the photographs of girls under the glass tops of the tables in the sitting room of the house we were occupying, and curious about the bells which had been fitted in each bedroom. How innocent we were. La signora explained that the bells, now silent, were set to ring at twenty-minute intervals when the peace-time business of the premises was brisk, and that the girls could still be brought over at short notice. We looked again at the photographs and declined.

And so, later, did the range of culinary and carnal pleasures on offer. On joining a weekly repertory company in Worthing none of the recommended theatrical digs had a vacancy. I found a room at 'The Firs'. Or was it 'The Pines'? When my wife came down unexpectedly for a night I asked would it be all right if she shared my bed and my breakfast. 'Where are your lines?' asked the proprietress. Lines I thought were what I had to learn by Monday. The lines she was seeking, however, were not related to Act III. Marriage lines were what she needed before she opened the door. Even then, long before the liberated sixties, my wife and I had never thought it necessary to carry them around with us, and it was only very reluctantly that, with no proof of the legality of our relationship, the dragon-lady allowed us in. She remained suspicious of me and later in the autumn informed me that she had 'stopped my little tricks'. I would find out what she meant, she said, when I went to my room. My little trick had been to light the gas fire on cold nights while studying the next play to be presented, and she had so entangled the gas tap in heavy-duty wire that it was no longer operable. Silly me. I should have known that gas fires were merely for decoration.

I left as soon as I could and took the precaution of explaining to my next potential landlady the nature of my work and my working hours. 'Perfectly all right,' she said. 'We're very bohemian here. We often sit on the floor.' I moved in, thankfully, to Liberty Hall but stayed too briefly to derive much pleasure from that particular freedom. A room at last became vacant at Number 11, Station Road.

Mrs Spratt was in one way very aptly named. She was not at all fish-like but she was very small. Mrs Sparrow. She prepared three meals a day for us, always ready on time. We were not, and often came back late at night to find her patiently waiting to serve supper. Every Thursday morning, when I was free from rehearsals, she turned on the geyser and ran a bath for me as I finished breakfast in bed. And all for £2 a week.

Mr Spratt was a slightly mysterious figure in the background, and it was a long time before we discovered what his work was. Unlike his wife he never came to see the play we were performing. Never, that is, until I played what critics would refer to as the eponymous hero in *The Man in Possession*. Mr Spratt came to see that – twice. And he declared it his favourite play. He, too, was a bailiff.

Conditions can change rapidly in the theatre. A year after moving into 'the Sprattery' my digs were very different. One week the address was 'Baur-au-Lac Hotel, Zurich'; another, 'Grand Hotel, Florence'; and yet another 'Hotel Negresco,

Nice'. Breakfast in bed was readily available every day of the week but no one ever turned on the geyser, and I always had to run my own bath.

That Bloody Woman Again!

INVERCARGILL is the last date before the South Pole. The theatre was built in 1892 and is part of the Town Hall. Backstage there are posters on the walls of the scene dock announcing seasons (of three days, which we did, too) of plays starring H. B. Irving, Lewis Waller, George Rignold, Oscar Asche, Julius Knight, Dion Boucicault, Marie Tempest, Irene Vanbrugh, Alan Wilkie and many more.

The main hotel, when we first went there in the middle fifties, was quite good except that there were no telephones in the bedrooms and people were paged to answer a phone call through loudspeakers, one of which was right outside our bedroom door. This, of course, prevented us from resting for an hour or two in the afternoon before the play at night – a lifetime habit.

I protested to the manager, but he said there was nothing he could do about it as it was the only way to contact the guests, and it might be for an important message. It was a quite impossible situation and we had decided we would have to leave and try to find another hotel, when John [husband John McCallum] found a remedy. He stood on a chair in the corridor when there was no one about, unscrewed the front of the loudspeaker, undid a wire – and we had peace.

After the show that evening there was an all-night party at the hotel – a staff party to farewell the assistant manager. Nearly all the staff were Maoris and at about 2am they embarked on what sounded like a series of war dances. John went down to remonstrate with them and they told him they would be winding up soon. They did, after about an hour; and then an hour later, just as I had got to sleep, I was woken up by someone putting something around my neck. I screamed, sat up and was astonished to see two very beautiful but drunk

Maori girls putting a garland of flowers around my neck. They had strewn the bed with flowers, starting at my feet and completely covering me. It was their way of apologising for the noise they had made. After the party they had gone into the garden, collected the flowers, strung them together, opened the door with a pass-key, tiptoed over to the bed, had quietly decorated me – and woken me up! John was very taken with the whole rigmarole.

When we finally got to sleep at about 5am it was at least with the knowledge that we wouldn't be woken up at seven by 'Phone call for Mr Smith . . .'

We had peace for the three days and nights we were there. The new assistant manager apologised to us for the malfunction of the paging system, but assured us that he would send a note up if we had a phone call – to be put under the door he said.

Three years later we made another tour of New Zealand and stayed at the same hotel in Invercargill. The paging system was working again, but John fixed it, and for the three days and nights we had peace.

Two years after that I made a tour of New Zealand without John, who was working on the management side of J. C. Williamson. The paging system was working. After the play, about midnight, when all was quiet, I took a chair out into the corridor, undid the front of the loudspeaker, as I had seen John do, and freed one of the wires. Peace for three days and nights.

Three years later I made another tour of New Zealand, again without John. When I arrived in Auckland I asked Tom Manger about my hotel bookings. The same hotels everywhere he said, except Invercargill. When he had phoned the hotel, the manager had said, 'I'm not taking that bloody woman again. Every time she comes here the whole paging system fuses and it takes days to put it right!'

Answering the Call

A N hour and five different sets of directions later, soaked to
the skin, his feet squelching in his shoes and his hands
blistered from the worn handles of the cases, Larry Gower
arrived at a small terrace of back-to-back houses, black and
unfriendly in the dim light cast by the street lamps at each end.

He rang the bell of No 3, apprehensive about his reception
and the lateness of his arrival. Wally had fixed the digs for both
of them, but he was not arriving himself until Monday morning from Sunderland.

A light went on in the window above him, and a few minutes
later he heard footsteps descending the stairs and then a
scuffling of slippers along the passage. A chain rattled, a bolt
slipped, and the door opened about three inches.

'Who's that?' snapped a hard, suspicious voice.

'It's me,' mumbled Larry inanely, then, remembering
himself, 'Larry Gower – Wally Winston wrote to fix for me
and himself.'

The door opened wider, revealing a vast bulk in a dressing-
gown. The light from the hall spilled over Larry's sodden form.
He was aware of being scrutinised as he stood hunched against
the driving rain. His fair hair was now plastered over his
forehead, and his round face with the black-rimmed spectacles
wore an anxious, owlish look.

'Come in, then,' said the flat nasal voice, devoid of sym-
pathy. Thankfully Larry picked up his cases and stepped
damply into the house.

He was in a narrow hallway, lined with framed photographs, which led to a flight of red linoleum-covered stairs.
The door slammed behind him and he turned to face his first
landlady. Mrs Rogers was huge, absolutely huge. Her hennaed
hair was crimped in curlers, and with her arms folded over her

tremendous bosom, and her woollen dressing-gown reaching to feet that were surprisingly dainty in fancy fur-trimmed slippers, she looked like Boadicea about to order her chariots into the attack. Her fleshy face was undistinguished except for a large, hairy wart just under her lower lip, and as she spoke it writhed as though it had a separate, sinister existence of its own.

'You're late,' she accused him. 'There's no supper for you, but there's a bottle of milk in the kitchen. Got your ration book?'

Larry nodded, vaguely frightened. After much fumbling he drew from his inside pocket a tattered ration book. She took it disdainfully, holding it with two fingers.

'This is your room,' she said, flinging open the first of three doors which led off the passage. 'Breakfast is at nine o'clock, in the kitchen.' Gathering her dressing-gown around her she swept up the stairs with all the dignity of a circus elephant.

Larry watched her go, open-mouthed, and then picking up his cases again he entered his room. When he had finally managed to locate the light switch, he stood in open dismay at what he saw.

It was a fair-sized room containing a brass bedstead in one corner covered with a greasy quilt, a wardrobe whose door swung open, a rickety bamboo table, and an armchair from the arms of which grey stuffing protruded obscenely. Apart from a raffia bedside mat, the floor was covered with the same red linoleum he had seen on the stairs. Here and there it curled up like the sandwich he had eaten at Crewe station. On the walls, shaggy Highland cattle browsed in ornamental frames and over the mantelpiece Landseer's *Monarch of the Glen* peered uncertainly through dusty, broken glass. On the mantelpiece itself stood a framed photograph of a Junoesque lady wearing tights and feathers and a wide false smile. This, on closer inspection, proved to be Mrs Rogers.

Larry grinned to himself. So she was an old pro then, he thought. Those majestic hams must have given many a stagedoor Johnny ideas. He thought of them now, how they must look, and shuddered involuntarily.

He undressed, shivering in the cold damp air. There was a gas fire in the room, but he couldn't get it to work, and he crept under the sheets, his skin shrinking from the icy contact. Blast! He hadn't put the light out. The bulb swung nakedly above the bed, taunting him, and then, as he swung reluctantly out of bed, he felt the urge to empty his bladder.

Wonder where the toilet is, he thought. Should have asked the old bag before she nipped upstairs. He went into the hallway and switched on the light, his stockinged feet sliding on the over-polished lino. The photographs on the wall trained a whole battery of theatrical smiles upon him. They were all photos of pros, all inscribed to Ma Rogers. 'Thanks for a wonderful week, Ma, Yours ever, Randolph Sutton,' 'Ma, I love your apple pie. Lots of luck, Fred Emney.' Double acts, who in real life never spoke to each other, posed with arms entwined; singers sang top notes in tail coats, and cross-eyed comics leered at each other across the walls, all welded together into one happy company – 'Ma Rogers' lodgers'.

Larry's need became more urgent as the cold began to seep through his thin socks and he gave up his inspection of the photos and concentrated on finding the toilet. He tried the door which led to the kitchen. The knob clattered under his hand and the door creaked open four inches – and stopped against an obstruction. He pushed harder and was rewarded with a low animal growl that chilled him to the marrow. In the half light from the passage he saw a huge tawny body lying across the door on the inside. An Alsatian dog looked up at him, teeth bared in a snarl.

'Good dog,' Larry croaked, offering a tentative hand. The dog moved its head sideways, watching him like a cobra about to strike. Larry wasn't very good with dogs; they had always had a cat at home, and even that used to bite him sometimes. The situation was desperate, his need was great, but he wasn't going to risk his manhood by stepping over this great lout of an animal. And, almost as important, he didn't want to come face to face with Mrs Rogers again. He mustn't make a noise, but somehow he must make water.

Shutting the door as quietly as possible he eyed the stairs. Perhaps there was a toilet up there? But that was where Mrs Rogers slept – he couldn't risk opening the wrong door. Those beefy arms could kill a man. Back in his own room again he searched frantically for a vase, a tin, a wastepaper basket – anything. There was nothing.

One solution remained. Open the front door and nip outside to the bushes. That's it, that's it, he repeated to himself as he padded up to the door. With trembling fingers, his face taut with anguish, he slipped the bolt, drew back the chain and opened the Yale lock. The rain hit him in the face through the half-opened door. He should go back for his coat, really, but hell, he'd never make it. I've got to go, I've got to go. He slid round the door and turning his back began to rid himself of his agonising burden.

The door blew shut behind him, the catch locking firmly into position.

With a light-headed feeling of inevitability he rang the bell again. The previous procedure of the light going on and the footsteps descending was repeated, only this time Mrs Rogers stood aside and motioned him inside wordlessly.

Larry forced a wet smile. 'Thought I'd have some fresh air.'

Mrs Rogers humphed and began to walk up the stairs again. On the fifth step she turned and in a grim monotone said, 'The toilet is the first door on the right at the top of the stairs.'

Larry slopped back into his room, frozen to the bone. Clawing off his soaking pyjamas he wrapped himself in the top blanket and crept miserably into bed. Mercifully, sleep came quickly to him. On the pillow his face without the spectacles looked strangely helpless and bereft.

from *Twice Brightly*

Food Parcel

MY story took place in 1952 while rationing still existed in the United Kingdom. Meat, of course, was a considerable luxury and my mother arrived at the Bolton Hippodrome where I was a new recruit, and indeed in my first job, not only with some particularly succulent sirloin steak but also with a bunch of asparagus. Both, at the time, great rarities.

I returned from the theatre after an afternoon rehearsal to be greeted by my landlady saying, 'Yer mam came dis afternoon, Mr Nimmo, and left sumthin' fer yer. I've cuked the steak and I've put the bluebells in water.'

Taking the Biscuit

NEVER go by the name of the house. The Waldorf turned out to be not the Waldorf Hotel but a piece of ground walled off and let as self-contained. I had never seen a 3-watt bulb before. Other digs were so cold that even the goldfish wore little scarves. One week it was snowing – in the airing cupboard. And the damp! In Ackers Street, Manchester, my room had wall-to-wall cress. In Wolverhampton it was ten shillings a night and pick your own mushrooms – off the wall. And sometimes you shared a room with more than two-legged friends. The first night I was in bed alone – thanks to the exterminator – or so I thought; but there on the sheet was a dead flea. I complained, to be told that I shouldn't worry about one dead flea; so I pointed out that later the mourners turned up. Some landladies had method. On a Monday they took off the pillow-cases, threw them against the wall and if they stuck, they changed them.

Barry Sinclair, who always toured the Ivor Novello parts, proved you should always make sure you know your room and exactly where the digs are. He once arrived after a hideous journey, threw his bags into his room and went off to the pub. After quite a few, he started back and took ages finding the house in the dark. He crept up the stairs, to be faced by three doors: which was his? He pushed one; it opened. He stripped in the dark and climbed into bed, stretched out an arm – and touched someone! Oh God! He gets dressed again quickly, can't find one sock, tries next door, turns on the light, bed empty, strips and jumps in. Next morning his tea is brought in by the fifteen-year-old daughter of the house, who says, 'Didn't hear you get in last night, and I sleep next door!'

Food in real digs wasn't always cordon bleu. Eddie Gray and Charlie Naughton of The Crazy Gang fame played

Southsea for two weeks, and for the first ten days every meal had been some small portion of fish. Eventually the landlady said that she would read Eddie's tea leaves. 'Aha, you're going to meet a stranger, Mr G.' Eddie said: 'I hope to God it's the bloody butcher.'

In Kettering, with *Charley's Aunt*, my digs had a lockless, outside loo. One day I was in there and heard footsteps coming down the path, so naturally I started whistling very loudly with the foot pressed firmly against the door – which was pushed and pushed until two hands were thrust round the side of it. In one hand was a shoulder of lamb and in the other a large piece of beef. A voice said: 'Which would you like for Sunday, Mr Blythe?' Well, I've ordered meals in some odd places, but that took the biscuit. I told the landlady how cold it was out there, saying I'd have sciatica in the morning, and she

IF YOU WANT TO KEEP PETS

said – honestly – I'd have Shredded Wheat like the others.

Of course some actors are pretty mean, too. I heard of one who used to give the landlady potatoes at the beginning of the week and tell her not to mash them. He wanted to make sure that he got back the same number he had given.

In Bath I was asked if I was the sort to entertain the opposite sex in my room at night, playing music and drinking till the early hours. When I assured her that I was not, the landlady said, 'Well I am, I hope you're a heavy sleeper.'

I am still trying to find the address of the digs where the landlady asked an actor if he'd like breakfast in bed. 'Don't bother,' was the reply. Later, if he'd like lunch in bed. 'No, don't bother.' In the evening, if he'd like steak and salad in bed. 'No, please don't bother.' And she said: 'Well I have to get up, I'm starving.'

IT'S A QUID A WEEK EXTRA!

Tournedos Rossini

THE front door bell doesn't usually ring before breakfast unless the postman can't get the letters through the slit. 'I'll go, darling,' I said as I sleepily descended the stairs in my dressing-gown.

It wasn't the postman. There were two of them in peaked caps and a dark blue Wolseley saloon stood beyond the garden gate. 'Police,' the one with the three stripes volunteered. 'Good morning,' I replied with as much cheerfulness as I could muster at such an early hour — well, early for me. 'Surely you can't want me to sing at your concert again?' He eyed me with contempt. 'Are you Ian Wallace of this address?' 'I am.' There didn't seem much point in denying it. 'Then I have to inform you that I have a warrant for your arrest on a charge of assault, and I must warn you that anything you say will be taken down and may be used in evidence.' 'OK,' I replied, 'would you mind if I have a mouthful of breakfast and a quick shave. I'm sure we can rustle you up a cup of coffee.'

'I wouldn't be too flippant if I were you, sir,' observed this rather mean looking twelve stones of Law and Order. 'You are on a serious charge and you're up before the beak at 10.30. Constable Trunch will accompany you upstairs to make sure you don't try to abscond through the bedroom window.'

What happened next was something of a surprise. I'd expected to be taken to the local magistrate in Archway Road, but the police car swung down Highgate Hill and headed for the city. 'Where are we going?' I asked. PC Trunch pursed his lips, licked his toothbrush moustache and then grinned like a hungry wolf. 'The Bailey, old sport!'

The judge had a face like wrinkled parchment from which glared piercingly blue eyes. His voice was high and slightly hoarse.

'You are charged with a vicious assault on a Mr Antonio Bombazino last night, the 10th of November 1949, at the Stoll Theatre, Kingsway, which took place on the stage in full view of the audience during a performance of Rossini's opera *The Barber of Seville*. How do you plead? Guilty or not guilty?'

'Guilty, m'lud.' I gave him a winning smile. 'Young man,' croaked his lordship, his face beginning to match the scarlet of his robes, 'not only do you admit to this dastardly attack, but you actually take pleasure in doing so.' 'Oh yes, m'lud, I'd been practising it on my lawn for two days.' 'SILENCE!' shouted the usher as a mild hubbub disturbed the calm of the proceedings.

'Ian Wallace, you do not seem to realise the seriousness of your situation. You come here without any legal representative and gleefully admit to assaulting a guest to our shores. You risk finding yourself behind bars for a very long time. I trust you are not going to plead insanity because in that case I shall double the sentence I already have in mind. Before I pronounce it, do you wish to say anything in mitigation?'

'Ah, now you're talking, m'lud, I thought you'd never ask.' He opened his mouth to admonish me but I got in first.

'Imagine yourself, m'lud, in the role of Dr Bartolo in *The Barber of Seville*. He's a crusty old lawyer, er, not a bit like you, m'lud. In Act Two the Count Almaviva, who is in love with Dr Bartolo's pretty young ward, Rosina, bursts into his living room disguised as a drunken soldier. The Count Almaviva last night, m'lud, was Mr Bombazino, the celebrated Italian tenor. During the scene Almaviva draws his sword and has a mock duel with Dr Bartolo, who only has a walking stick with which to defend himself. Very soon the stick is knocked out of Dr Bartolo's hand and Almaviva threatens Dr Bartolo with the sword.

'Last night, m'lud, I was singing the role of Dr Bartolo. The way we had rehearsed the opera did not involve Mr Bombazino brandishing his sword any nearer my stomach than six inches. Nevertheless at the previous performance not only did he touch me with the sword, he penetrated my costume and I felt a momentary pain.

'At the end of the act I returned to my dressing room to change my costume, only to discover that he had drawn blood.'

There was a murmur of interest in the public gallery and I suddenly had the full attention of the jury. For the first time Signor Bombazino, who had for some reason been allowed to take up residence in the witness box, removed the smug smirk from his olive-tinted visage.

'When I protested to him, m'lud, in my halting Italian, he merely sneered and suggested that I wait until the next performance. Then he added with a nasty laugh, "Maybe I killa you, eh?" I think it was meant to be a joke, m'lud, but I wasn't taking any chances. For the next two days I worked out a plan of campaign and practised it, as I told you, m'lud, on our back lawn with my wife gallantly volunteering to play the part of the Count Almaviva. So when last night Mr Bombazino drew his sword and gave me that mocking smile, I knew exactly what to do. I appeared to stumble and as I lurched forward I knocked his sword out of his hand with my stick and completed the manoeuvre by bringing my elbow in violent contact with his Adam's apple. I'm afraid, m'lud, that for the next ten minutes his rendering of Rossini's music sounded like a broody hen with croup.'

'Silence in court!' yelled the usher. Bombazino shook his fist at me. 'Well, m'lud,' I added when the mirth in the public gallery had subsided, 'wouldn't you have done the same in my situation?' 'Certainly not,' he cried, 'I'd have kneed him in the groin and made him sing soprano for the rest of the evening! Young man, I cannot overlook such disgraceful conduct. You will go prison for ten years. Take him away!'

As the goaler seized my arm a bell rang and the judge smiled happily. 'Ah, luncheon is ready, the court is adjourned.' The bell stopped but the goaler kept shaking my arm. I looked round to remonstrate with him to find that he'd turned into my wife. 'Wake up, darling. You're going to be late for rehearsal if you're not careful,' she said.

Although the court scene was only a dream, the events described in my plea of mitigation actually happened, more or less, nearly forty years ago on the stage of that fine old theatre and opera house that used to stand at the Aldwych end of Kingsway on the left-hand side going south.

In subsequent performances Signor Bombazino never let his sword anywhere near my abdominal region, relieving me of the necessity to cut off his splendid *bel canto* in self-defence.

Bastien on Tour

WHERE was our golden labrador puppy, Bastien, amidst all those to-ings and fro-ings? With us, of course. He was now huge and for most of the tour he had been suffering from a disease called hard pad. One conventional vet said he would have to be destroyed – so we took him to a vet who believed in homoeopathic treatment. Each day Bastien was given various pills and potions, fed on a diet of fish and clad in a little green woollen jacket. He survived – but not before he had been sick over Elspet and me in the car during an inter-city journey (even our best friends wouldn't come near us for a time after that – a pretty kettle of fish!) and had caused tumult by twice tearing open pillow cases, when left alone in our bedroom, because he was too ill to be taken to the theatre.

The first time he did this was in Blackpool. The landlady was an horrendous creature who terrified us all and rationed her hot baths as though the war was still on. '*One* bath per week *each*' read the notice – hard by 'God Bless This House'. '*One* bath per week *each*. No more than *five inches* must be run. *6d extra per bath*. DO NOT use the bath before permission has been obtained. Vim is provided at no extra charge. LEAVE THE BATH AS YOU WOULD EXPECT TO FIND IT'. So you paid your sixpence – entered the freezing cold bathroom to be confronted by a chipped, stained bath and a geyser which could have doubled for a Wurlitzer Organ. You turned on an assortment of taps, the mighty machine groaned and wheezed into life and out came a dribble of tepid, rusty water. Five inches? You couldn't get in *three* before the damned water was stone cold anyway. It's the only time I've ever tried to bath in cold iron-filings. At least my bottom was scoured clean by bits of enamel and old Vim.

By this, you will gather that we were somewhat in awe of

our gorgon landlady. She'd looked askance when we'd taken Bastien along – but we persuaded her that his green jacket and need for smelly fish made him quiet and docile and really he was just a lovable lap-dog. Grudgingly she admitted us and him – with dire warnings of immediate ejection if so much as one dog hair mucked up her already filthy house. We meekly concurred – and Bastien was duly installed with his bed made in our large suitcase, and off we went to the theatre.

On our return for our joyless supper, we first looked upstairs to check on Bastien. Horror upon horror. As we entered the room feathers floated and billowed up from all corners. Bastien greeted us wildly – certainly he'd done a good job – and the threshing of his tail adding to the chaos already abounding. We slammed the door – all thoughts of our cold cod and chips downstairs forgotten, and spent the entire night catching and collecting feathers, then stuffing them back into the torn pillow case. As dawn came up over Blackpool's treeless streets, we were completing the Herculean task. Elspet was reinforced in her belief that Bastien should go (she'd already tried to give him away – but I sulked so much he was brought back) or our marriage might well be in jeopardy. Fourteen years later we were still together and Elspet lovingly held poor old Bastien's head as he was put to sleep.

from *My Farce from My Elbow*

Bed & Bath

'TWENTY-FIVE shillings all in,' she said. It seemed alright to me. I had thirty shillings a week from the theatre; this left me five bob for myself.

'We haven't got no bath,' she said, 'but you'll get a good breakfast, and we'll see you're alright.'

'Er . . . good,' I said.

'Call you at eight?'

'Right.'

Eight o'clock, a knock at the door. Mother and sixteen-year-old daughter carrying a huge bath. The bath was placed beside the bed. Jugs of steaming water followed.

'Your ablutions, Mr Pleasure!'

I thanked them.

'Cleanliness is Godliness, Mr Pleasure! Eileen will be back,' she said.

I waited. Sponge, soap and bath towel laid out on the bed. Eileen had not returned. My bath was getting cold. I slid into the comforting water. A quick knock, and enter Eileen with breakfast: eggs, bacon and lots of buttered toast. She slid a small table over and placed the tray beside my bath. 'Do you enjoy a good soak?' asked Eileen.

'Oh yes,' I said nervously, reaching out for the toast and letting the butter drop down my chin. She waited. 'If you don't need anything else?' I gulped hot tea.

'See you tomorrow morning.'

'Er . . . yes,' I said, hopefully.

The best digs I've ever had.

Scarpering the Letty

ONE of the most bizarre events concerning digs happened to me during my second week in show biz – back in nineteen hundred and mind-your-own-business. I had joined a knock-about variety act known as The Crazy College Boys. It consisted of a middle-aged man, who ran the act and played the headmaster in the schoolroom sketch (which was a kind of down-market Will Hay), two other teenagers, a dog, and two dwarfs. The dwarfs, like the rest of us, played pupils in the sketch and the dog was toured in order to work one gag. This consisted of the dog walking across the stage from one side to the other with a 'prop' head fixed to its rear end. This gave the impression of a two-headed dog and used to get a big laugh.

The second week of my tour with this act took us to Swansea Empire. As we were all getting around £3 a week we were staying in the same digs, which were supposed to be paid for by the Guvnor. On the Saturday night, about three in the morning, I was wakened by a heavy hand on my shoulder and a voice hissed in my ear, 'Get up, we're scarpering the letty.'

In my boyish innocence I thought that this was some Latin phrase with show-business connections. Not having encountered it before I said, 'We're doing *what?*' The Guvnor said with some impatience, 'We're leaving without paying. Hurry up!'

And a few minutes later we were all leaving through the kitchen window! The Guvnor, the three boys, the two dwarfs, and the dog. Two weeks in show business and I'm a crook already! If a certain Swansea landlady should happen to read this, even if she is a hundred and two, I will be happy to send her the week's rent.

Three of the Best

I never had the pleasure of a theatrical landlady; most of them were far too old. In any case I have never been on a theatrical tour far enough from home to require a bed for the night. It was always a case of curtain down, a quick glass of Nigerian Riesling, into the car and away.

I suppose Gladys Adams could qualify as a theatrical landlady. And Kitty Cox. And Carole Thomson. Gladys and Kitty were a couple of Cardiff housewives who gave me shelter and solace in my days with the BBC Welsh Drama Repertory Company. Gladys's house was at the posh end of town: Roath Park, not to be confused with the nearby area with the unlovely name of Splott, which sometimes pretended to be Roath.

Before Gladys, I had endured some dreadful landladies – grim, intolerant old bags, cartoon characters, identical down to the last whisker. Gladys Adams worked for the local department store where I sometimes helped out between broadcasts. I was her first lodger, and probably her last. The first night I was there, I missed my last bus home from Treforest, where I was visiting a pair of sisters. At dawn, as I tiptoed up the staircase, Gladys appeared in the kitchen doorway. I braced myself for the onslaught – 'My husband never behaved like this and I won't take it from the likes of you' etc – and indeed Glady did let rip. What she bellowed was, 'Oi, you dirty old stop-out. What do you want for breakfast?'

So began a wonderful relationship. She was a warm, dynamic creature, with flashing eyes and a bosom that cast a shadow over her feet. The household was completed by her teenage sons and daughter and the fearsome Nan. Nan was the prototype for Giles's Grandma in the cartoon series, white of hair, black of brow, and savage. She was known affectionately to the children as the Old Hag. Amazingly, in her late seventies, she fell in love and became a different person, and would embarrass me with accounts of her carnal activities.

Years later, when Eamonn Andrews fell upon me with 'you thought you were just having a quiet night out . . .' Gladys Adams was there, drawing me to her famous chest and reminding me of the happiest months any young radio actor ever had. (Sadly, by this time, Nan had gone with her lover to the great Boudoir in the Sky.)

Kitty Cox's place was in Canton, which, in spite of its name, is a suburb of Cardiff. Kitty, too, was jolly and broadminded. She and her husband, Stan, ran a happy home, full of noise and what they liked to think was music. Kitty sang many songs, but always with the same lyrics: 'True lovers meet again.' She wore a grey curl in her red hair, and stockings with birds in flight up the thigh. Stan's hair was cut in the Kirk Douglas style, and he sported a blazer with the badge of the Pioneer Corps fashioned in gold braid. Between them, in fun and hospitality, they gave me far more than I paid for.

Carole Thomson was perhaps the best qualified. She was a landlady, and she was certainly theatrical. When I stayed at her north London home, I was working as a television news-reader at Alexandra Palace, and Carole was earning fees as a freelance gypsy violinist. She and her two sisters, Cammie on piano and Marie on drums, had once been the Calores Sisters, cabaret artistes and stars of *Workers' Playtime* on the wireless. Their parents were Italian immigrants. Carole was in the Gladys Adams mould, with a 'hear no evil' philosophy. To her, everyone was a nice boy or girl, regardless of age. I could do no wrong, even though I tried. The only thing that worried Carole was that my bed might not be big enough.

Weekends were one long Italianate celebration, which were extended in summertime to three-week visits to the Old Country, myself included in the party. Reunions with the girls' aged relatives were tearful; I cried too, and I had never even met them before – such was the strength of emotion.

My wife is an actress and has done the traditional touring

bit; she has suffered or relished the company of some characterful landladies, including the legendary Alma McKay of Manchester, who no doubt has been written of elsewhere. I'll drink to Gladys, Kitty and Carole. For a small consideration, I might even give you their address.

Stranger in the Night

IT was early days, and I mean early days, probably about five or six weeks after my first professional date. I didn't have a car but that didn't matter because I didn't have much luggage either, so I used to turn up at the station of whatever town I was appearing in and start searching for the cheapest digs available. Sometimes it was very difficult because most places had been booked by mail or whatever before the commencement of the week.

On this particular occasion I arrived in Barrow in Furness, where I was appearing at Her Majesty's Theatre. This was on a Sunday about lunchtime, prior to the show opening the following day. I searched all the afternoon and most of the evening without success. I was just about all in when I went into a pub, where an old man who listened to my hardluck story gave me an address where he said the lady used to take in boarders up to a couple of years ago. I left my battered suitcase at the pub and, by this time, almost limped off to the address provided, rang the bell and waited anxiously. A grey-haired elderly lady answered the door with an old-fashioned oil lamp in her hand. I doubt if she could afford electricity. I explained my situation and beseeched the use of a room for the week. She contemplated the thought, then, leaving me at the door for several minutes, she returned and agreed that if I would come back in not less than an hour's time, she could accommodate me. I went back to the pub and spent that time and may be a couple of bob feeling much more contented, and I thanked the old man. I was fixed up with digs for the week.

By the time I left the pub it must have been around 10.15. The necessary hour had soon passed and I almost skipped with my luggage to what would soon be bed.

The lady answered the door but this time not only did she

have an oil lamp in one hand, but a lighted candle with a box of matches in the holder in the other. We scaled two flights of stairs and then she showed me into a small room at the back of the house with a single bed. There was an old wooden box which was obviously intended to stand in for a bedside table, on which I put the candle. I undressed, laying my clothes on the floor – there was no alternative – and then got into bed. I was so tired I almost hurt my ear on the pillow which, in any case, wasn't all that soft, and then – dammit! I hadn't been to the loo. I didn't want to have to get up in the middle of the night, and besides, she hadn't told me where it was.

Then it occurred to me there might be a chamber pot, or po as it was then called, under the bed for such purposes. I leaned over in the dark and felt underneath. My hand contacted something strangely cold, but so far, no po. I thought I'd be sure so I struck a match and leaned over further to look under the bed. My head hit the floor with shock as I almost rolled out of bed. The strange and cold object was a body!

I must then have created a record worthy of entry into that illustrious Guinness Book, because in just a few short seconds I had packed, and with the suitcase in one hand whilst dressing with the other, I descended two flights of stairs extremely rapidly – I don't remember opening the door – and disappeared down the street. May I add without paying the bill.

Having gone to the Police Station to report the incident, they invited me to stay with them for the night. Their enquiries revealed that the lady's husband had died a natural death the day before and that she had managed to get his body, which was awaiting the normal undertaker's services, under the bed in order to facilitate a comfortable night's rest for me. Who knows, perhaps the expected fee could have been some inducement. Even these days though, whenever I see a po . . . my God!!!

The Mystery of Edwin Drood

AFTER a period of portraying a certain Scottish Medical Practitioner, I found myself – only to pay the taxman, mark you – involved in a production touring company of *The Mystery of Edwin Drood*, adapted by, completed by, produced and directed by the impresario himself, from Charles Dickens' unfinished last novel. It had been said that the impresario concerned would not divulge the source of the completion, but was of the opinion that the quality of the writing was superior to all of Dickens' works put together, and he had given the company the luxury of a full eight and a half days' rehearsal.

In cahoots with a young woman of the apple cheeks and ample bosom, so favoured by the great man (Dickens), and after the consummation of our relationship (while rehearsing our lines in her flat in Chalk Farm), we compiled together an advertisement. This we had circulated in the local press of the towns and cities in which we would be appearing over a fourteen-week period. If my memory is faithful to me, it was worded thus:

THE MYSTERY OF EDWIN DROOD BY CHARLES DICKENS & CHARLES BLOGGS is being given at the . . . Theatre . . . on . . . Mr W. (Bill) Simpson (DR FINLAY) who plays Edwin Drood, and his wife [she *was* playing my wife] seek suitable accommodation with comfortable surroundings in a homely atmosphere ('A wee cup of tea, Doctor?').
Please reply to Box . . . .

You would be amazed at the offers of hospitality which poured in from ladies in towns as far apart as Kirkcaldy and Aberystwyth, some enclosing photographs of JANET lookalikes, begging us to come and spend the week – for no charge

– sampling their bannocks or laver bread, according to the delicacies which the locality threw up.

We would arrive at our diggings on a Sunday in the 1928 Wolsley, specially loaned to me by a friend, in a town like, say, Peterborough, to find that the house which was to be our little love-nest for the week was in the courtyard of the cathedral and occupied by one of the vergers and his lady wife.

Doctor Finlay's car was no Rolls Royce, and it didn't take a stethoscope to listen to the timing of the engine. Our arrival needed no heralding by the carillon of cathedral bells which greeted us, and within no time at all doors and casements were being thrown open and rotund Dickensian figures – mostly clad in black – were appearing to ascertain the source of the hullabaloo.

'Oh, William!' cooed the little pouter pigeon in the passenger seat, with the plaid shawl around its pretty knees. 'It's just like Edwin Drood,' and she gave me a look of lust and longing which had no place in the courtyard of a cathedral, but confirmed in Edwin Drood's crotch the conviction that underneath the souciant plaid there lay that which would ring all his bells that very night. 'Oh God!' I thought, as my eyes followed the Heavenwards tracing of the ringing spires, 'how would *you* have finished it, Charlie? I hope you're up there somewhere, because I'm going to share this one with you. Please be my guest. I'll try and make it as funny as possible and *you* can be in the cupboard!'

We were welcomed into the house by a beaming lady with subservient gestures and a strongly Scottish – but to my ear unconvincing – accent. I held the door for little Miss Pouter Pigeon and she passed in. As I moved to follow her, I felt the draught of Dickens pass in behind her. It was a cold draught, but unmistakably Dickensian. Only a claw-hammer coat could have made that kind of draught, and only snuff could have scented it. I sneezed involuntarily. 'Bless you!' beamed Mrs McCatchit, leading us upstairs.

The room looked out over the courtyard to the cloisters and contained the usual bedroom furnishings, which regarded the large brass bedstead with disapproval.

'I hope you'll be comfortable,' cooed Mrs M. 'Afternoon tea will be ready downstairs in half an hour,' and she rustled out.

I found myself examining the cupboard as Turtle Dove unpacked the suitcase. 'Oh William,' she sighed, clasping her hands together under her chin, 'isn't it romantic?'

'I think it's as close to Heaven as I'll ever get,' I said, eyeing the cupboard, removing her hands from her chin and raising them to my hungry lips. She was as sweet as rose petals and flicked out her little tongue to receive me. 'Damn tea!' I thought. However, before we went down I took out a flask of whisky from my overcoat pocket and placed it on the mantelpiece, which was adjacent to the cupboard.

The verger, or whatever he was, waited downstairs by the fire and the scones and cakes and tea cosy – which bore a discreet resemblance to Mrs M., appearing from the kitchen with a plate of toasted muffins dripping with butter.

'Mrs Drood' then gave us an excerpt from Act 2 Scene 3 of the play, in which she enthuses over the presentation of a Christmas dinner prepared by her aunt. I cannot be certain, but although she managed skilfully to substitute the words 'scones, cakes and muffins' for 'goose, stuffing and plum pudding', I fear that Christmas pies crept in at one point of her eulogy. Mrs M., looking to the table with some puzzlement, was about to protest, but it was too late as Mrs D. had already skated cleverly over her mistake of identity and was giving us three pages on the delicate flavour of the tea.

The McCatchits were enthralled by this appreciation of their efforts and declared themselves to be charmed by the sincerity of a guest who was a member of a profession not noted for that particular virtue.

Thanks to this brilliant prologue, afternoon tea went off and was over in no time, ending before the fire had died down, with empty plates and drowsy, desultory and empty conversation. Therefore nobody protested when I professed that the drive from London had exhausted me and could I be excused. Mr M. also admitted that the unaccustomed excitement of the day had induced in him an almost uncontrollable reverie. Mrs D. offered to help Mrs M. with the washing up, an offer that was accepted, much to my impatience. However, I went upstairs and entered the bedroom.

There was an unmistakable smell of Scotch whisky in the air, and on the bedside table there was a leather-bound volume of *The Mystery of Edwin Drood*.

That night I slept fitfully through what seemed to have been a different lifetime, and when I was awakened next morning by the cathedral bells pealing through the open casements, I *knew* how Charles Dickens had ended *The Mystery of Edwin Drood*.

It all reminded me of the elderly thespian who was asked by an enthusiastic lady journalist after having seen his 'Hamlet' in Harlow New Town, 'Do you think that Hamlet actually slept with Ophelia?' He thought for a moment and then whispered nostalgically, 'On tour, yes. In the West End, never!'

Panto Time

IN a lifetime of theatre I've appeared in at least thirty panto-
mimes, and occasionally, I must admit, disasters have
occurred.

The first pantomime I can remember was 1943. I was fourteen years of age, and had just left school, when my father
arranged for me to play the cat in *Dick Whittington*, in his
production at the Empire Theatre in Greenock. I was directed
to follow the Principal Boy everywhere, and if she looked at
me, I was to say 'Miaow'. I faithfully obeyed all instructions
during rehearsals, until she turned unexpectedly one day and
nearly fell over me. Evidently, despite years of experience as
Principal Boy on stage, she was not expecting me to be at her
feet in the bar next door to the theatre. Our relationship
deteriorated from that point onwards.

The following year I moved up in the world and played the
giant in *Jack & the Beanstalk*. A wooden frame was made to
support me – three feet high and surrounded by tin, with straps
on the wooden top to insert my feet. The tin extended about
three inches above the level of the platform where the straps
were placed; the slightest tilt was accentuated and the tin had
the painful habit of digging into my ankles. Like most stages,
this one had an uneven surface and trying to walk on it was a
continual hazard to life and limb. I also burdened myself with
three large overcoats to help make the giant's body bigger, and
sported a beard. And I carried a prop cudgel about two feet
long and shaped like a large ham, which was, needless to say,
quite heavy.

One night, during the fight scene with the Principal Boy, I
nearly ruined the pantomime. She had a beautiful sword, I
only had my cudgel. Unfortunately, in my enthusiasm, I took a
swipe, caught her sword, and it finished up in the centre aisle of

the stalls, narrowly missing some of our better-paying cus-
tomers. This left Jack without any means of attack. However,
being quick-witted, the Principal Boy kicked at my boot until I
collapsed in the giant's chair, presumably with a poisoned toe.

I asked the director if, in the finale, I could walk on wearing
a very smart suit and carrying one of the giant's boots, just to
let the audience know who I was. But he insisted that as I had
been killed two scenes previously, this was out of the question.
So, on the last night, feeling the injustice of it all, my theatrical
training broke down. I attacked the prince with even more
vigour. I threw the cudgel at him or her, and followed it with
my beard, the giant's cloak and the three overcoats. The
audience was collapsing with laughter, which only served to
encourage me, and the director was collapsing at the side of the
stage, which I felt was his just reward.

One night at the Alhambra Theatre in Glasgow, in the
middle of *Sinbad the Sailor*, starring myself and David
Hughes, who later made a great name for himself in opera, the
fire curtain, which is held up by water pressure, began to
descend very, very slowly. The reason for this was a leak in the
overhead pipe which carried the water to maintain the curtain.
The orchestra scattered, clutching their music, as the water
had been in the pipe for at least fifty years and could not be
described as clean. Luckily enough, as the production was
'Sinbad', all the chorus, sixteen in number, were equipped
with mops which they used in one of the dance numbers. So
while they dried up the stage and the iron curtain kept coming
down, I did the only thing I could think of.

Backstage was a wonderful man whose job was called, in
those days, the property master. He had been at the Alhambra,
which was one of the great theatres of Scotland, all his life, and
was now in his seventies. I grabbed the bewildered man, still in
his brown overall coat, and took him on stage. We stood at the
front microphone, just clear of the fire curtain, where I did
what I can only describe as 'This is Your Life'. I got him to talk
about some of the great names of the theatre that he had seen
on stage and worked with. It took about fifteen minutes or so

for the fire curtain to be raised again, but the audience didn't seem to mind. They appreciated that what they were hearing was theatrical history and something exceptional.

This brings me to one of the greatest variety theatres in the world, which I had the honour to play on more than one occasion – The London Palladium. I was booked for my first pantomime there with Englebert Humperdink and Arthur Askey. I was the first Scottish comedian for sixteen years in that position, and to say I was nervous would be a considerable understatement. Arthur Askey, of course, was tremendous to work with and had years of experience. His warmth and the audience's feelings for him personally were quite unique. He may have been small in size, but on stage he was a giant personality, and I was thrilled to be in a show with him.

As the opening night drew nearer, we were all of us nervous and tense. Engelbert Humperdink was a very nice fellow to work with and extremely professional. Alan Curtis played the baddy and I don't think there is anyone better in that role in British theatre. The production was again *Sinbad the Sailor* and included in the cast were the Dingbats, a wonderful group of acrobats with split-second timing. For their spot the stage had traps built in the floor, so that when they threw themselves on the ground they would fall straight through to a specially prepared mattress underneath. They were all dressed in costumes identical to those worn by Arthur and myself, to give the impression that we were coming from all parts of the stage at once. All Arthur and I had to do was a bit of business to get it started, then keep well out the way until we appeared at the end of the routine to carry on with the pantomime.

On the final run through on the opening day, I could see the twinkle in Arthur's eye as he was enjoying the build-up to this comedy scene. Because of this I think he was distracted, and he rushed into a danger area and fell down one of the special traps. He was jammed by the mechanism and obviously in great pain. An ambulance was called and he was taken to hospital, where he had to stay for ten weeks. Later on I went into my dressing room and found the director there with some of the other artistes, insisting that we would have to cancel the performance. The idea of coming all the way to London from Scotland and then being cancelled, even for one night, was too much. I said, 'Wait a minute, Billy Tasker's his understudy and he's an old pro – he'll know every word.' And I was right. Billy and I had a very quick run through of odd little bits as there was no time to do anything else.

The curtain went up. The audience was already feeling down after the announcement that their favourite star was unable to appear, but, somehow or other, the show worked. Not as good as it would have been with Arthur, naturally, but certainly up to The London Palladium's standard. Three-quarters of the way through the second half I rushed off stage to hear a voice saying: 'Engelbert can't make the change.' Without hesitating, I turned round and was back on stage at the microphone in the greatest music hall in the world without a thought in my head, without a joke that could fit the situation, but opening my mouth and rabbitting on. After an eternity, which was really only a few minutes, Alan Curtis joined me and we did what in music-hall parlance is called a bit of boo and hiss. Alan, of course, was very experienced – we didn't need any rehearsal for this – and we got the audience all worked up without them realising that we were just filling in. I then got the signal from the side that everything was okay again, and we made a hasty exit.

It was only at the end of the show, when the curtain had fallen, that I realised what I'd had the cheek to do. I vaguely remember my agent saying to me sometime during the run, 'I think they're going to give you a sport's car or something as a present, because you kept things going.' I do remember not getting whatever it was, but in the end that wasn't important. For that one moment in my life, I shared a very special experience.

Fire Hazard

IT was my third week in the magic world of show biz and I was appearing at the Royalty Theatre, Chester. I was still under the impression that I was Terry-Thomas reborn and despite the slight handicap of my thick Leeds accent, I was convinced that my dove grey suit, pearl waistcoat, cigarette holder and carnation would achieve the illusion. The stage manager – a winning soul with bad breath and hush puppies – enquired whether my carnation was 'fire-proof'. Upon my expressing ignorance as to its condition, he produced a cigarette lighter and set fire to it. The resultant damage to the entire lapel led to a frantic search of Chester for an invisible mender.

In the interval between the two shows that night, I was invited by other members of the bill to join them in the circle bar for a drink. Thrilled by this acknowledgement that I was a real professional, I accepted. As it was a hot summer night, I decided that cider was a good idea, unaware that the brand in stock was Merrydown. I remember consuming five. When I attempted to rise to return to the dressing room, my legs would not, at first, comply, but otherwise I felt in fine fettle.

The climax of my act was a joke I had stolen from the great Max Miller. This always saved me – as my performance up to that point was usually greeted with a mixture of disbelief and utter incomprehension by the good burghers of whatever town I was appearing in. This particular night, the joke was received in complete silence. I sang my song and left the stage to the sound of my own feet.

Upon enquiring of the stage manager – the arsonist of earlier in the day – what he thought may have gone wrong, I was informed by him, with some relish, that I had told the joke twice. In direct succession. I had finished it and started it again. This episode is carved on my heart, just below 'Skegness is so bracing'.

Seeing Triple

DURING the mid-seventies, when every town it seemed had its own cabaret club, we, The Brother Lees, would work at such clubs for a week at a time, so good digs were always a top priority. We had a policy to invite the landlady to see the show as soon as possible because, if she enjoyed it, the rest of the week at her guesthouse would be far more pleasurable – with guaranteed late breakfasts, cups of tea on request, all the factors that contribute to a successful stay.

On one such occasion we were staying with this Irish landlady in Warrington and, sure enough, she accepted our invitation to see the show on the Monday night. We gave her the best table in the room, and wined and dined her. She seemed to be enjoying the show immensely, laughing in all the right places. It was during the time in our careers when we were concentrating on our triplicate impression routines – three Max Walls, three Tommy Coopers etc – for programmes such as *The Generation Game*, and the landlady seemed particularly amused by these. After the show, we went over to her table and asked her the 64,000 dollar question: 'Well – did you enjoy it?'

You can imagine how we fell about laughing when she replied, in all seriousness, and in her broad Irish accent: 'To be sure I did, but why this club bothered to book the three of you when one could have done it, I shall never know.'

Life's Little Luxuries

THE cliché is true. There is nothing so cold, wet and dispiriting as a north country seaside town in November. But, as the door opened, the house seemed cheerful and the welcome warm.

'Take your cases up and then you'd like some supper. I've got a little luxury to cheer you up,' she said.

But one approaches 'digs' like an experienced hunter; the undergrowth can be dangerous, and so it proved. The rooms were chilly and the beds were damp – not damp, wet – if a match were lit some sort of spontaneous combustion of marsh gas might occur; even the pages of *The Stage* lining the chest of drawers were yellow and limp. Oh well, what was seven nights in a pullover and overcoat, there was a little luxury to come – undreamt of cordon bleu!

Sometimes you enter a room and there is some eccentricity, some strangeness that you cannot grasp, some echo of doom. The sitting room seemed pink and chocolate in colour. What was it? There were table lamps everywhere, not two but thirty-one. Each had a pink shade and the bases were smiling, polished, chocolate gentlemen; a harlequin, a jack-in-the-box, some in moorish robes, some in loincloths, some plain indiscreet. Stranger still, none of them worked, no bulbs, plugs or points, only yards of flex, each neatly folded and secured with an elastic band. We felt outnumbered, last ditch defenders at Rorke's Drift, afraid of laughter that might be returned with sepulchral war cries and flashing assegais.

In came the baked beans on toast, as cold and wet as the bedroom mattresses. She smiled. 'Have you noticed? Chocolate's my favourite colour. Everyone wants my lamps but you don't get a collection like this in a day. Don't you think the pink shades set them off – my "boys" I call them.' She stopped short of giving each one a personal introduction, but after a short family history and a sigh of affection, said as an afterthought, 'No fires, it spoils the shades. I'll bring your little luxury.' Back she came and there, under a British Railways glass dome, were three chocolate eclairs. There was hope! They looked magnificent, sparkling brown, cream oozing from their sides. 'There you are, enjoy yourselves,' and she was gone.

Once again, as hunters, we stalked our prey. Off with the dome and all seemed well. But no, we sensed trouble. They say the Rock of Gibraltar is permanent, so were the eclairs – petrified Gold Medal Winners at The Great Exhibition of 1851. Nothing would shift them. Even a concerted rush with three forks produced nothing but a few shavings of igneous pastry; they were inviolate in their sculptured grandeur. 'You lads and lasses are like children,' she said. 'Like to keep your surprises,' she beamed, as she cleared the table.

Of course we 'played' every night that week and so did the eclairs. No surprise was shown and they were whisked away for the next 'performance'.

It was bitterly cold on Saturday night. We decided to rebel, forego the baked beans, the assault on the eclairs; smuggle in fish and chips and, what is more, to light the fire. No chance! The damp *Stage* drawer-liners defied the matches. But wait! There they were, the petrified buns still lurking beneath their odeon dome. They looked sadly sacrificial transferred to the grate awaiting their fate. Would they light? The 'thin brown line' held steady for a moment and then broke. The cream and pastry liquefied over the *Stage* repertory notices, flared and flamed. On went the coal from the polished scuttle; paradise regained!

Suddenly she was back, wrinkling her nose. 'What's those bangy noises?' – 'We've lit the fire' – 'What with?' – '*The Stage*'.

She seemed uncertain for a moment, but her 'boys' were smiling and the only oddity was the empty glass dome. She scanned the room like Carter looking for Tutankhamun's

Tomb, and then admitted defeat. 'Hope you enjoyed them,' she said. 'Yes,' we said.

What a pleasure a small victory can be. Every lamp seemed to be lit. All thirty-one.

When You Have To Go . . .

THE only digs we stayed in during several tours of New
Zealand in the fifties and sixties were in Oamaru and
Timaru, towns on the east coast of the South Island, and very
good they were too, but many of the hotels in the small towns
in those days were very like digs. One of them turned out to be
particularly disappointing after a long and dusty drive. We
were travelling with Joanna, aged four, and Nanny who had
come from England with us to look after her.

When we arrived at the hotel we were shown into two very
small rooms at the back, overlooking a yard. As the hotel was
on the sea front and we had booked several weeks in advance, I
went down to the office to remonstrate with the manager. It
turned out to be a woman, who said she owned the place; she
was extremely unhelpful and antagonistic, saying that she had
had some actors staying at the hotel before and if I had any
other complaints to make she would send her husband up to
see me – and he was a professional boxer.

I climbed the stairs wearily knowing there was nothing else
except to put the bags back in the car and try to find somewhere else to stay, when I was met on the landing by a
mischievously smiling Googie [wife Googie Withers] who
said, 'Come and see what I've found.' It turned out to be a
small suite facing the sea and consisting of two bedrooms, with
a bathroom between, and a sitting room. What's more, she
and Nanny had carried the bags in and had started to unpack
them.

'We asked for the best accommodation they had,' Googie
said. 'This is obviously empty, and so we'll have it.'

I knew it would be only a question of minutes before the
gorgon downstairs appeared, accompanied by her bruiser husband. I just had time to get out the whisky bottle and pour a

couple of stiff ones before the door burst open and, predict-
ably, the first words she shouted were, 'What the hell do you
think you're doing in here?'

As she swept into the room, eyes blazing, I was glad to see
there was no ominous large shape looming behind her. But she
was formidable enough by herself and the way she ordered us
to vacate was in the best tradition of parade-ground sergeant
majors. 'I've had a Williamson head girl here before,' she said
(we worked this out later as being a reference to Gladys
Moncrieff, Australia's leading musical comedy star who had
often toured New Zealand for J. C. Williamson's – as we were
doing). 'And she hung her washing all over the rooms and spilt
a bottle of red wine on the carpet, which took me weeks to get
out, so I'm not having any more of you in here.'

But she had met her match in Googie, who simply sat
looking at her and said, 'We booked the best accommodation
and we'll have it.' The owner/manager took a step towards
her. 'If you touch that chair, let alone my wife,' I said, 'it will be
assault and I should think a six-month minimum sentence.'

'We'll see about that,' she said. 'I'm sending my husband up
to see you.'

Half an hour later he arrived, obviously prisèd out of the bar
where he must have spent the last few hours. If he had ever
been a professional boxer it must have been as a bantam
weight, because he was about five foot two inches tall and in
no shape at all to undertake anything pugilistic. In fact, he was
at the stage of being deliriously happy about life in general and
well disposed to everybody, including us. He readily accepted
a glass of whisky and in no time at all was telling us what a hell
of a life he had with his wife. He left about an hour later, telling
us not to worry and that everything would be alright. And
indeed it was – until about three o'clock in the morning.

We had performed the play, had supper, and we were all
asleep – that is except Joanna, who was half-asleep. She had
woken up, wanting to go to the loo. The little mite had a vague
idea of the geography of the 'suite' from what she had seen of it
the night before, but in the dark she had overshot the

bathroom door, turned sharp left and taken five paces which a ready reckoning told her was where the pedestal was – and woke me up with the sound of splashing water next to my bedside table, and all over the carpet.

Well, we washed it, we scrubbed it, we poured soda water on it, we put an armchair over it – and then packed our bags, crept downstairs, left a cheque, and went on our way to the next town before dawn.

Milligan and the Monkey

ALTHOUGH I have no personal experience of living in theatrical digs, I was once in the position of affording accommodation to a theatrical idiot (purely in the professional sense), to wit, Spike Milligan.

During the late forties I was not only script writing for BBC Light Entertainment, but also proprietor of a Westminster hostelry that bore the family name, having been established by my great-grandfather a century earlier.

'Grafton's', as some may recall, was a watering hole for many on the radio scene at the time and I have fond memories of after-hours carousals with Tony Hancock, Dick Emery, Alfred Marks, Bill Kerr, Norman Vaughan, Robert Moreton and other contemporaries. Above all it was the birthplace of 'The Goons', as a collective entity. Peter Sellers was both client and friend, as was and is Michael Bentine. Mike introduced me to Harry Secombe, with whom I have, as the song says, been together now for forty years. It was Harry who introduced me to Spike and thus set up a chain of circumstances that led eventually to *The Goon Show*.

This, then, is the setting for the incidents I shall describe. Spike, who set out as a trumpet player and occasional comic, felt that an additional outlet for his talents would be comedy script writing, and how right he was. However he was, at the time, without an adequacy of either literacy or funds. Harry prevailed upon me to take Spike in for a few weeks to help remedy both deficiencies. With a wife, two children, an invalid aunt and staff to accommodate, the only room left for Spike was the attic, in which was already housed our pet vervet monkey, Johnny.

Any trepidations on my part (I can't speak for Spike) soon disappeared as we all began to enjoy an hilarious time together. Spike's comic inspiration began to find expression in our joint radio scripts and he formed an affectionate relationship not only with my small children, who still remember his stories of the 'Hobbly-Gobbly' men, but also with Johnny, who responded to him almost as a kindred spirit. Certainly there was a marked similarity in the shifts of mood from quiet introspection to manic, darting-eyed activity, mischievous from Johnny, comedic from Spike and unpredictable from both.

We wrote mainly at night, often with Johnny as the only witness to our ourbursts of argument or laughter as scripts took shape. At other times he slept on an old sheepskin coat in a large cage, clutching a rag doll from which he hated to be parted: Johnny that is, not Spike. On outings to the park he frolicked on the end of a longish rope which allowed him to climb the occasional tree, but indoors he was allowed a rather risky freedom, sometimes wreaking havoc by finding his way into the kitchen, where Spike insists he once saw him add his own water to the soup; a suggestion indignantly denied by our head cook, Louie, of fond memory, who had great affection for the little monkey and in later years was to visit him regularly in his final home at Chessington Zoo.

What is true is that someone, maybe Spike, but more likely my young son, put Johnny in the service lift and sent him down into the bar during opening time, which nearly gave the waitress a fit and caused great mirth amongst the clientele. On another occasion he escaped from an upstairs window with Spike valiantly trying to retrieve him by crawling on to the window ledge, to the delight and catcalls of the throng below.

The other Goons were not free from involvement, Harry and I once finding ourselves, somewhat merry after a lunch party, trying to explain to a policeman what Johnny was doing causing chaos and confusion in a nearby greengrocer's shop. The monkey was not our only pet at the time. We had Siamese cats and a young bulldog as well. Johnny used to fight with the cats, usually on top of somewhere, since they were all climbers, and occasionally ride on the bulldog's back with encouragement and help from Spike. The dog, Buller, was equally playful and liable to get excited. Harry once, in a fit of exuberance, performed an arabesque over Buller, who leapt vertically upwards and seized Harry's upper and inner thigh. The nearest, as Harry put it at the time, that he had ever been to 'losing his wedding tackle'. Johnny was not averse to taking a quick bite at the odd finger, which led Harry to make a joke of retracting his hand into his sleeve, limping and saying, 'I've just been to Jimmy Grafton's place.'

I have always suspected Spike of being concerned with Johnny's *pièce de résistance*, which was as follows. From time to time after a broadcast we would retire back to the pub for some after-hours relaxation. On one such occasion, Robert Moreton, one of the principals of the show Spike and I were writing, *Hip Hip HooRoy* (in which Spike's famous character 'Eccles' was born), was sitting in the bar below the stairs leading from the upper regions. Bob, best remembered perhaps for his 'Bumper Fun Book', was, like many comedians, privately somewhat lugubrious. He also wore a fedora hat of which he was very fond. Johnny was, in the interests of harmony and peaceful enjoyment, not normally privy to such gatherings, but somebody (was it Milligan?) opened a connecting door and suddenly there was the little money perched immediately above the unsuspecting Robert. Animals sometimes react nervously to sudden noise. The acclamation of Johnny's presence may have startled him into action, or he may have had something against the Moreton hat. Anyway, he proceeded to pee all over it from, as they say, a great height. Bob, surprised and swearing, snatched off his beloved fedora, but Johnny hadn't quite finished and the remainder was received bareheaded.

Were we all unkind to be doubled up with laughter? I don't think so. We laughed a lot in those days. We've laughed a lot since; but whenever I picture the days when Spike was our lodger, the monkey is there beside him.

Star Terms

IN the mid-thirties I was on a provincial tour with a play called *Red Night*, prior to opening in London.

In the cast was Robert Donat and a marvellous comedian called George Carney. Bob Donat and I had been staying in hotels and George in theatrical digs. He convinced us that we were squandering our money and that we could live very cheaply and in great comfort if we followed his example.

George booked us all into rooms in Blackpool, run by a rather forbidding lady called Mrs Maypole. We had quite an

enjoyable week, the food was reasonable and there was a fire in the sitting room when we returned from the theatre. The one slight misadventure was that the bath had been newly painted with green paint which, unfortunately, had not quite dried before I luxuriated in hot water and found that I was firmly glued to the bottom of the tub!

On the Sunday morning of our departure, George asked Mrs Maypole for the bill. She produced a document of alarming length which seemed to be the best part of a yard. George produced a pencil and went slowly down the columns; when he reached the total, a look of apprehension clouded his face. He looked up at us and said in a small voice, 'Who had butter?'

The bill was astronomical by his standards. It seems that Mrs Maypole had made a special price for 'film stars'.

Drop of the Hard Stuff

DURING a theatrical tour of the mid-western towns of New South Wales in 1950, we found ourselves staying overnight in a small country pub. At two o'clock in the morning a flood warning came through. We had to get out of the area immediately or be stranded. I went down to the bar, which was packed with the local residents. Behind the bar stood the publican; his face resembled a relief map of old Ireland. He was wearing an old singlet with a lump of rope round his waist to hold his trousers up.

I asked him if there was anything in a bottle we could take with us, to which he sadly replied, 'No, Ed, the beer truck didn't get through.' I said, 'There must be something.' Looking furtively around he said, 'We've got some local steam here if you'd like to give it a whirl.' I said, 'What's it called?' He said reverently, 'Rare Old Tawny Aldringa.' After a second's pause I said, 'Is it any good?'

Fixing me firmly with his eye he replied, 'Listen, Ed, when you knock the bloody top off of that you can hear the grape-pickers quarrelling!'

My Theatrical Kennel

IN 1953 I was about to go to Scotland to start location filming on Walt Disney's *Rob Roy, The Highland Rogue*. I asked my secretary to book rooms for me at the Buchanan Arms Hotel at Drymen. I was specific about my requirements: I wanted a double-bedded room for my wife and myself, a twin-bedded room for our little boy and his nanny, and a single room for me as a dressing room without any bed but with cupboards or hanging rails for my voluminous Highland wardrobe.

My secretary telephoned the hotel and made reservations which were accepted, and then added, as an afterthought, that I would be bringing two of my dogs, a Great Dane and a corgi. The receptionist then informed her that no dogs were allowed in the hotel, so my secretary cancelled the reservations as she knew I would not travel without these two dogs.

Within minutes the phone in my office rang. It was Mr Charles Guy, the then owner of the Buchanan Arms. He explained that there had been a mistake and that *of course* I could bring my dogs. He explained that he had dogs of his own at the hotel, and that there had often been trouble with guests who had ill-controlled animals, but that he was sure that my two would be models of decorum.

So my reservations were re-made.

On my subsequent arrival at the hotel I found everything perfectly in order in the two double rooms, but was annoyed to find that there was still a single bed in the small dressing room, leaving very little floor space.

When I complained about the mistake at the reception desk the disarming reply was, 'Oh, but Mr Todd, where will your dogs sleep?'

So much for NO DOGS ALLOWED!

Flashback

ALTHOUGH my performance as Viola in *Twelfth Night* is to this day etched in the memory of my form master, never having trod the boards professionally I am barely qualified to contribute to this collection. Nevertheless, as an itinerant Outside Broadcaster I can claim during the past forty years to have hung my hat on a strange peg or two. Indeed Anthony Hopkins, the musicologist not the actor, has seen fit to publish one such shared experience associated with the BBC coverage of the Le Mans 24 Hour Race during the late fifties. At least he had the decency to enquire prior to publication whether or not I would sue him – 'After all, one is still a gentleman', as my dear late friend John Bolster remarked at the time.

Bolster will be fondly remembered by enthusiasts as Our Man in the Pits, when 'the pits' was an expression associated exclusively with motor racing rather than tennis stars, the President of the NUM or Mr Rupert Murdoch, depending on one's point of view.

Having completed our broadcasting duties at some French motor race or another, and I forget which it was, John and I found ourselves within striking distance of Paris, but too far from the Channel to catch the ferry. Fred Payne's Bar beckoned, and we heeded the call. From 'Fred's' we went on to 'Roger's', 'Roger's' to 'La Fifinella', 'La Fifinella' to 'La Moroque' and so on and so on.

Dawn was breaking when we entered the modest Hôtel La Paix on the Left Bank, where le patron had never failed to provide us with accommodation at no notice flat at whatever time of day or night.

All too soon, and greatly to my surprise, I was wakened by

the distinctive voice of my friend in the adjacent bed of our shared room.

'I say, Waymond,' he said, 'is that you?'

'Of course it is, you clot,' I muttered. 'At least I think so. Why?'

'Oh thank heaven for that,' he said. 'Look at that.'

'Look at what?'

'At the door,' he croaked.

There hanging from a hook was the most disreputable flasher's mac ever to have been presented in court as Exhibit A. Every limp fold of it was obscene.

'For a terrible moment,' said John, 'when I saw that thing, I thought I'd weally overdone it this time. Shall we wing down for a glass of champagne with our coffee?'

The Hat Stand

WHEN I was young and innocent and my ears were bigger than they are now, I worked as a teacher in a small North German town.

It had its municipal theatre, of course, and many of the minor luminaries and aged thespians from there rented rooms in the lodging house found for me by the school.

Our landlady was a formidable creature.

I guess she was in her late thirties and her gold teeth were somewhat older.

She had a figure like Kim Novak and a face like an imploded pomegranate.

She had an endless variety of gentlemen friends, and when entertaining one, she would hang his trousers on the hatstand in the hall.

It was like Buckingham Palace displays a standard when the Queen is in residence or the House of Commons flies its flag when David Dimbleby is taking tea there with Esther Rantzen.

I was terrified of the landlady.

I was young. I was innocent. And I had only two pairs of trousers.

Sometimes she would walk unannounced into my room when I was taking my breakfast of hard-boiled eggs, slices of sour German grey bread and a bottle of beer.

She would put her hands on her hips, look me up and down (which didn't take very long) and say:

'Ach, Herr Tinnisvooot, you are so thin. Have you the stamina for it?'

'The stamina for what?' I would say.

And she would sigh and say:

'I must remind you, Herr Tinnisvooot, that young ladies are not allowed in the bedrooms of my gentlemen guests. Please remember that.'

I would nod my head and blush.

One week a symphony orchestra came to town. It was from England and a section of the woodwind players was billeted in our lodgings.

On the morning before the concert the landlady came into my bedroom and said:

'Herr Tinnisvooot, tonight I entertain the gentleman bassoonist. Please to tell me all you know about Menchester.'

I did, and she smiled to herself.

I felt I should warn the bassoonist of his impending fate.

I did, and he gulped hard and said:

'Bloody hell, I'd better find a floor to sleep on for the night. Ta very much, lad.'

He had nicotine stains on the bridge of his nose. He wore his trousers at half mast.

I went to the concert in the evening. I went to the reception, too, to act as one of the translators.

The bassoonist sought me out, and I told him everything I knew about the landlady.

He gasped with horror, particularly when he saw her smiling at him from the other side of the room.

'Ta very much, lad,' he said. 'You've saved me from a fate worse than death. I'm sharing a room tonight with the trombonist with buck teeth.'

It was late when I got home that night.

I had spent the hours drinking beer with the head of the English department, Professor Smiss, who was the only man I've known before or since to possess a Nansen passport.

He was from Estonia and couldn't pronounce his 'Th's'.

Neither could I by the time I got home to the lodgings.

I let myself in carefully.

And there facing me on the hatstand was my other pair of trousers.

There was a light in my bedroom.

I went in.

The landlady was lying naked on my bed.

She opened up her arms to me and said: 'Herr Tinnisvooot,

Menchester is a city situated on the rivers Irwell and Medlock. It is a centre of cotton manufacturing industry and has a unique swing bridge which carries the Bridgwater Canal over the Menchester Ship Canal.'

Later, much much later, she whispered in my ear and told me that Karlsruhe was the centre of cement making in Bavaria.

Home on Wheels

TO be on hand while doing this [Morecambe and Wise's] first television series, Eric, Gail and I had moved into yet another rented house, this time in Acton, again for a three-month period. Renting a house also made it easy for us to have our families come and visit us. But towards the end of this time we had one of our less successful ideas.

'Let's buy a caravan,' we said. 'It'll solve all our living problems,' we said. 'A home on wheels that we can tow from place to place, etc, etc.'

We had been inspired by the fact that Stan Stennett had always managed caravanning beautifully. We forgot that at one time he had driven lorries and was extremely useful as a mechanic. Why, Stan could even fly a 'plane. We could just about drive a car. Nevertheless, we bought one.

'Intrepid' being our middle name, off we drove to Manchester for a week's work in variety, the caravan hitched to the back of our Austin Hereford. We only broke a couple of cups on the way there, and collected just a wee knock on the van's nearside bodywork. The next problem was: what do you do when you arrive and there's nowhere to park? We couldn't drive round Manchester indefinitely. Finally the theatre allowed us to come to rest on a piece of waste ground near the Stage Door.

It was one of those weeks of torrential, incessant rain that I thought only happened in comic stories about Manchester. We were confined to the limited space of the caravan, with nappies piling up that couldn't be dried, until we looked for a mobile laundry. One morning I put a casserole in the calor gas cooker for our lunch. When I opened the oven door to check on the cooking, I noticed that the gas had blown out. Not thinking, I struck a match to relight it. There was a fearful explosion and I hurtled backwards. The blast was strong enough to lift Gail in her high-chair several feet but, mercifully, she was quite unhurt – just a surprised look on her face! Little flames, meanwhile, were darting about the top of my head. Help! My hair was on fire. I managed to beat them out before too much damage was done, but couldn't quite save my eyelashes. They were now little singed stubbles.

About half an hour later it hit me that there could have been a real, dreadful disaster. Suppose I hadn't opened the oven door for some while, thus allowing the gas to build up. It would certainly have been the end of 'Morecambe & Wife'. Well, not Morecambe. He was in the theatre. When he did turn up and stepped into the caravan, he didn't know whether to laugh or cry. He simply said: 'And who are you?'

When it came to caravanning, practice did not make perfect. All that business of getting it hooked on to the towing bar – and how do you get the wretched legs to stand level? Is it really supposed to list to one side? Why are the plates sliding off the table? Even the daily routine of pulling out the beds and putting them away again, plus not having hot water on tap and proper sanitary arrangements – all this might have been all right for a short holiday on a well-equipped camping site, but not for the busy life we were leading.

Apart from one beautiful summer, when Gail was getting on for two years old and we had a site near the beach at Squire's Gate, Blackpool, caravans did not work for us. Probably our worst experience was the journey we made from the North to Birchington, not far from Margate. We had broken the back of the journey without a hitch and were feeling very confident and relaxed. Then, somewhere in the vicinity of Elstree, we were confronted by a hill which, even to look at, made our hearts sink. Eric quickly changed into second gear and I clutched Gail a little tighter. Then disaster. Halfway up the hill we came to a halt and started to roll backwards, but with a caravan on tow you don't go back in a straight line. The caravan did this beautiful jack-knife across the road, and thank God there were no cars immediately behind us.

However, I could see a steady stream of traffic coming up the hill; soon they would be with us. It was then that I decided to abandon ship, still with Gail in my arms, and take up traffic duty.

The other cars got the message all right – perhaps because I was yelling like a demented fishwife and brandishing a baby to get the point home. (Whatever became of my fashion training – elegance at all times?) In the nick of time, and red with embarrassment, Eric put the car into first gear, managed to straighten up, and off we went, feeling more than a trifle foolish. We always said that whatever we did was tinged with comedy, and it was true. So much for caravans.

from *Morecambe and Wife*

Bed Bugs

M Y first theatrical tour took place at the ripe old age of
seventeen. I was then a student at the Royal Academy
of Dramatic Art; Sir Kenneth Barnes, the Principal, decided in
his lack of wisdom that the population at large should have
culture stuffed down their throats, in the form of two one-act
plays by Thornton Wilder and Anton Chekhov. Twelve
students, including yours truly, were designated to perform
these two extremely obscure plays to bemused provincial
audiences. One of these audiences consisted of members of a
Highland Regiment. I can still hear their cries of 'Awae hame
yer sassenach bums!' Needless to say, apart from getting the
bird the length and breadth of the northern half of this green
and pleasant land, I also encountered two landladies of
dubious merit. One amorous, the other an extraordinarily
dirty lady who on reflection bore a remarkable resemblance to
Les Dawson in drag.

The amorous landlady resided in Grimsby. She too was no
oil painting. Her loving hints fell on deaf ears as far as I was
concerned. I was a virgin at the time and in my own somewhat
moralistic way wanted to save my first attempt at physical
contact for Miss Right. Miss Grimsby of 1943 had other ideas.
One dark and misty night she crept into my bedroom, slipped
into the bed, took her teeth out and cried, 'Come on, kid, let's
go!' I protested vehemently, feeling absolutely revolted by the
thought. A look of disgust crossed my would-be paramour's
face, 'Oh,' she said, 'you're one of those show-business poofs.'
At that time I was not particularly interested in preserving my
macho image. I considered that any form of escape was better
than none, so I took her cue. 'Yes, I'm afraid I am,' I lisped. She
muttered as she left my bedroom and judging from some of the
remarks she made they were more than libellous about my

manhood. Incidentally, some time after I did lose my virginity to a Glaswegian stripper who left me with a souvenir of our night of love, but it soon cleared up with treatment!

It was on that same eventful theatrical tour that I met my Bristolian Les Dawson look-alike. Unlike Miss Grimsby, this one *never* put her teeth in, and I am delighted to say she had no amorous intentions. However after bedding down for the first time at her establishment, I awoke some two hours later with an indescribable itching pain. I got out of bed and turned on the light. The bed, the walls and indeed me, were covered in bugs. I called out hysterically to the landlady. She came rushing into my room. 'Look at these bugs,' I cried wildly. 'Oh dear,' said Miss Dawson, 'isn't that terrible, you must have brought them in with you.'

For once in my life I was speechless. I suppose I should be grateful she didn't report me to the RSPCA.

Ham and Egos

SOME fellow actors claim that theatrical digs no longer exist. Well, I'm here to tell you they still do. The names have changed and the prices have gone up, but the stage doormen of most provincial theatres will furnish you with a digs list. Some will even tip you the wink on how to avoid nylon sheets. What stays constant is the perverse desire of the majority of theatrical landladies to chat into the night. They give no thought to the poor actor who has just given a performance for two or three hours and has probably had to dash, still wearing his mascara, into the nearest hostelry with less than ten minutes to spare in which to sink seven or eight pints.

Landladies usually like to talk about *other* actors, and this frequently induces boredom. Was it Michael Wilding who said you can always recognise an actor by the glazed expression that comes over him when the conversation veers away from himself? Well, Michael should certainly have known!

Another hazard for the touring actor is the obligatory inspection of the guest book. Names, patently false (Nellie Nestle, the condensed soubrette comes to mind), going back to Irving's day are produced, pointed at and pronounced upon at considerable length by the proud hostess who claims the famous have passed through her lowly portals.

Actually, the worse moment is when she asks you to have your photograph taken. Bored, glazed and not infrequently reeking of alcohol, one has to stand with one's arm round her neck, beaming insanely at her ancient Brownie which takes what seems an hour before the flash goes off. There's a place in Bournemouth where the theatre vicar was (and maybe still is) improbably named Julius Caesar. One is invited to a very nice lady's house for afternoon tea and to play croquet. The afternoon is always topped off by the dreaded photograph.

Landladies are a little broader minded now. They accept television as an entertainment medium which is here to stay. Manchester's legendary Mrs McKay typifies the changing attitude. In the late fifties and early sixties she didn't much care to accommodate 'television artistes' (always pronounced by her as art*eests*) because they weren't 'real actors like you get in the Theatre' (The-Ater). But once Granada really became established and *Coronation Street* became the living newspaper, she started to prefer the telly lads because they could pay more.

Betty Porter, who lives in Blenheim Place, Brighton, is a smashing landlady with a curious custom. She takes only one guest at a time, but instead of payment, she insists on a red plastic rose to which she attaches the actor's (or actress's) name – and which, of course, lasts forever. If you visit her a second time, you have to give her a *blue* plastic rose. I assure you they're hell to find. I haven't been back a third time yet, but I'm hoping I will be able to. Presumably she makes it very difficult and you have to get one specially made. Purple with green spots or something. As a matter of interest, she has a complete patio garden which grows nothing but plastic.

George Jerome, incorrigible rogue that he is, isn't a Catholic or Jewish so far as I know, but he does like to make things awkward for his landladies. One Friday night, he held up a piece of meat with horror and said with the true tragedian's tremolo, 'Is this ham?' and his landlady riposted, 'At which end of the fork?'

Arriving one Monday morning in some bitterly cold Northern hell-hole, George realised he wouldn't have enough cash to pay his digs that week. So he went to the local hospital, found a spare bed and pretended to be a patient. He had noted the name – McClusky – of an ancient and very unconscious gentleman in Ward A and took the clipboard from the bottom of his bed, transferring it to his own bed in Ward B. He got three meals a day and crept off to the theatre on Monday evening for the performance. But on Tuesday he had to go to the theatre in his pyjamas because the nurses had confiscated his clothes. He was very late for the Wednesday matinée however because McClusky, whose identity George had assumed, died. The Company Manager only just got him out of the crematorium in time for his first entrance in the play.

Overseas digs are different. For example, they're usually in warmer countries than England. That's my experience. Somehow I don't fancy a twelve-week tour of Greenland. Being warmer, strange things can happen. On a world tour with the Old Vic in 1961, David Dodimeed, a tall, athletic actor with a beautiful voice, was sunbathing on the roof of his digs in Brisbane, Australia. I should add he was apparently sunbathing stark naked. He got bitten by a mosquito. Guess where? Well it blew up out of all proportion and he had to wear a splint on it. I leave it to your imagination what he looked like in tights.

After a ten-year gap, during which I was locked up for much of the time in television studios, I went back to touring with a vengeance about three years ago and have been a rogue and vagabond ever since. I started to go back to digs and discovered they really haven't changed much in the thirty years I've been an actor. Mornings of staring glassily at a plateful of black pudding and greasy bacon and eggs and wishing the Alka Seltzer didn't fizz so loudly. I tend to avoid the after-show 'in house' suppers by dining out. Hopefully the landlady will have gone to bed by the time I get in.

However, early in 1986, I got caught out rather badly on the late homecoming score. The landlord and landlady with whom I stayed in Birmingham had a private bar, to which they invited a lot of apparently very thirsty friends. To avoid the inevitable 'I know the face but . . .' and 'What do you do for a day-time job then?' and 'All actors are a load of poofs', I ate out and crept in late. But each succeeding night, no matter how late I returned, they were always up waiting for me. So on the Friday night, I stayed at another hotel and didn't return to the digs until eight in the morning. Damn me, if they weren't up preparing a wedding breakfast!

What – No Digs?

IT would be somewhat difficult for me to write about my experiences in theatrical digs, because I have never been in any. I have done no professional acting, and would certainly not be good enough if I tried. I confine myself to the amateur stage. But I do recall one episode in which digs would have been useful. It happened a long time ago – it must have been around 1947 – but I will not forget it.

Normally I appear on the stage for one week per year, in the local pantomime. Nowadays I live in Selsey; in 1947 I was in East Grinstead, and we used to put on our shows in the Cloth Hall, which has long since been pulled down to make way for a ghastly office block. That year we also took our pantomime to Tunbridge Wells; we were raising money for the local school for handicapped children. As usual, I played the Demon King (I specialise in demons). On the Wednesday we did a matinée, and then an evening performance. At the end I was rather slow in going to get changed, and when I did I made several interesting discoveries:

1 My everyday gear was in a case, which had been taken on the coach bringing us over.
2 The coach had departed for East Grinstead, blissfully thinking that I was going home by car (as had been originally mooted).
3 My car was in East Grinstead.
4 All the trains had left.
5 There was nobody around to give me a lift.

By the time I had worked all this out there was almost no leeway. Either I caught the last bus, or else I didn't. I took the plunge, made my way to the bus station and went on board. My appearance, in brilliantly green make-up and wearing a black cloak and beard, would have excited comment in any case, but the fact that I was also wearing horns and a tail made

it worse. Two women uttered loud squeaks, and one scrambled hastily off the bus before I could explain.

During the homeward journey, which lasted for an hour, the reactions of new passengers picked up en route were mixed. Some did their best to ignore me, while others clearly thought that I was an escapee from the nearest bin. I was rather glad to get home.

It wasn't a trap into which I fell again!

Shades of Novello

THE nearest I ever came to staying in digs was a place in Leeds, belonging to a Mr Basil Hartley, an avid Ivor Novello fan, who owned two houses side by side, frequented by 'entertainments' people. These houses, divided into numerous bed-sits, were named Novello House and Villa Novello.

The first time I stayed there Basil showed me round. He talked a lot about the great days when Ivor had been there, and obviously things had not been the same in the theatre *since* the days of the Novello shows. It was both touching and sad to see Basil's continuing devotion.

Over the years people who stayed had left photographs which lined the walls of the light green rooms. As he showed me my room, Basil indicated the photographs and said in his gentle Yorkshire accent, 'You won't feel lonely here, Mr Pigot.' Indeed, I recall that as I fell asleep I could see the street lights glinting in the glass of the pictures. It was like going to sleep 'with a full house'.

The Good Old Days

A few years ago I was presenting a rather startling act from
Holland – Joe Andy. His act consisted of, among other
tricks, climbing a high ladder situated in the stalls, while
balancing two swords, point to point. (If you have ever
thought in the past that this is a mechanical trick, read on!) Joe
Andy wished to combine his TV appearance with a few days'
holiday, and he came to Leeds three days early. The poor
fellow contracted 'flu, and stayed in his hotel taking antibiotics
prescribed by the theatre doctor. No one, including Joe Andy,
had considered that the side effects of antibiotics can cause a
slight dizziness and lack of perception. Joe's rehearsal created
an incident such as I never wish to see again.

He went through his juggling trick without difficulty, and
started to climb the ladder with the two swords point to point.
When halfway up the ladder there was a slight slip on one of
the rungs, and a flash of a sword as it flew down and into the
raised face of the Dutchman. I immediately feared it could
have pierced his eye, and with thick cotton wool pads to stem
the prolific bleeding, he was rushed to the General Infirmary.
About one and a half hours later he returned, his eye heavily
padded, and with the news that the point of the sword had just
missed his eye, but badly cut the eyebrow and eyelid, and
twenty-five stitches had been inserted. It seemed obvious that
he should withdraw from the programme with a return date
when he was fully recovered, but true to the form of a seasoned
circus artist, he insisted upon presenting his act that same
evening. No amount of persuasion could change his mind, and
– as he sensibly pointed out – if he did not go back immediately
and perform this hazardous trick, he would never have the
nerve to do it again.

The actual show was tense and dramatic. His eye pad was

removed, and the stitches were quite visible on camera. Leonard Sachs made a rather emotional announcement, and Joe Andy climbed his ladder, balanced the two swords as if nothing had happened, and came down on to the stage amid tumultuous applause. A true professional, and a very brave man.

Top Town was the forerunner of a highly successful international programme, *It's A Knockout*. Both programmes owe part of their success to the inclusion of amateur performers who all worked together as a team. If *Top Town* had been merely a talent-spotting contest, there would have been no room for police choirs, folk dancers, brass bands, schoolmasters and undergraduates, all of whom entertained as a hobby, with no thought of professionalism.

Occasionally unforseen hazards occur in amateur shows. A young man in a team from Hartlepool sang *La Donna e Mobile*. His normal accompaniment had been a piano, and although he started the aria a bar behind the orchestra, he carried on quite oblivious to his mistake. Alyn Ainsworth, the conductor, stopped the orchestra, allowing the piano to synchronise with the singer, and then the orchestra resumed in the same tempo as the singer.

Afterwards, I expressed my regrets, and hoped the singer had not been too embarrassed. 'Embarrassed?' he said. 'If the orchestra had played *Alexander's Ragtime Band*, I should still have sung *La Donna e Mobile!*'

On *It's A Knockout* one of our remarkable games was eventually vetoed by the then Managing Director of BBC Television, Sir Huw Weldon. The game was simply called 'Piano Smash', its object being for four strong and able men to smash an old disused piano into small pieces with the aid of sledgehammers. The debris was then to be pushed through a six-inch aperture, and the whole area swept clean in the shortest possible time. The speed at which some competitors could demolish an instrument was alarming.

Strangely enough, while it may be possible to devise similar games, such as breaking up old sideboards or dining tables, the result is not so compelling. A poor old piano makes such strange sounds as the strings jangle and clang, and it is fascinating to see the keys and hammers flying in all directions. This game became not only an important ingredient in the programme, but an on-going challenge to all teams to beat the existing record.

Sir Huw Weldon said this was debasing an object of intrinsic artistic value, and we were asked to refrain from including it. Reluctantly, therefore, we removed this popular feature, which had a rather unfortunate 'behind the scenes' drama at a seaside resort which will remain anonymous. It was the general practice with this game to rehearse the team on old pianos which local residents were often only too pleased to be rid of. Many old pianos had been obtained for the event and were stored in the care of the Local Authority of our anonymous seaside resort. On this particular occasion, members of the team were sent to bring out the one remaining rehearsal piano, as the Press had arrived to take pictures. This was their first visit to the council premises, but they saw a piano in a back room and promptly transported it to the rehearsal area.

Just as the sledgehammers were about to descend on the instrument, a frantic cry from a distraught official revealed that the piano which had been brought out for the demolition display was none other than the pride of the council – a rosewood Bechstein! Maybe it was just as well we had to discontinue the game.

It was during a Blackpool Summer Season that I tried a very unusual gimmick in the presentation of *Stars At Blackpool*. Morecambe and Wise were appearing at the Central Pier, Bob Monkhouse and Denis Goodwin at the Winter Gardens. Both double acts were comparatively new, but just beginning to establish themselves. I decided to put both acts on the same bill, but the twist would be in billing and presentation.

The situation would be developed so that Ernie Wise would

suggest that Bob Monkhouse would make a better partner than Eric Morecambe. Eric Morecambe would indicate that he would be happier and funnier with his new partner, Denis Goodwin. In the course of the sketch everything would be resolved, and the original partners reunited. The gimmick was to be the *Radio Times* billing. This was to read 'Morecambe & Goodwin' and 'Monkhouse & Wise'.

Everyone agreed on the idea, both for material and eventual billing, but we came across a stumbling block – indeed, two stumbling blocks. Both the agents of the acts disagreed with the idea and felt it might do harm. Consequently it fell through, and both acts appeared on *Stars At Blackpool*, but on different programmes!

A number of years ago there was a very talented Austrian performer called Hans Soffer. He presented a delightful 'cocktail time' piano act, in which his broken accent and leisurely piano style made him a great favourite, especially with the ladies. He gave a short series of late-night programmes called *Hans at the Piano*, in which the set was simple and the presentation relaxed.

Although a most distinguished looking man, Hans was unfortunately a little bit thin on top, and this was accentuated by the strong lighting of a TV studio. In those days late-night programmes did not warrant a make-up assistant, and a 'Do-It-Yourself' kit was left out for the solo artists to 'powder down'. The one problem in the programme was the shine from the head of poor Hans, but we had an extraordinary studio manager, John Day, who loved handling any situation. John therefore came to the rescue, and said the only way to overcome the problem was to match up some sort of make-up material with Hans Soffer's dark hair. To my consternation he produced a tin of black Cherry Blossom boot polish!

When faced with a live programme and limited rehearsal time, anything goes, so on went the boot polish. The result was a perfect match, a resplendent head of hair, a happy Hans, and a very 'polished' late night show.

Chest Mike

MY first working trip to Australia was in 1973. I was doing a play called *The Mating Game* with an Australian cast, and one of the girls in the play had to run around in bra and pants. The actress playing this part was extremely well-built and very short-sighted – she didn't wear contact lenses so everything must have been blurred, to say the least.

Anyway, one evening during the performance when we were playing a scene, and she had been rushing around as directed, she turned to me (in bra and pants) and I was amazed to find her half out of her bra! She obviously couldn't *see* what had happened and didn't seem to be aware that anything was amiss! I then had the problem of trying to tell her what was wrong without (a) stopping the play and (b) causing her acute embarrassment, and possibly hysterics. So when I got the chance, which seemed to be ages, I said to her under my breath: 'Your chest mike is showing,' whereupon she calmly looked down, squinting, and replaced the right boob – then carried on as if nothing had happened!

This event took place on several other occasions during the run of the play, and I merely had to say 'chest mike' for the escaping boob to be returned to where it belonged.

Getting Your Ration

WHEN I toured the variety theatres in the early fifties, food rationing was still in force and if you were on full board then the first duty on arriving in digs on the Sunday night was to give the landlady your ration book and hope for the best.

If she had an 'understanding' with the local grocer, butcher, or whoever, then you'd eat well. If not, well, hard cheese (literally) and better luck next week. If you catered for yourself, on the other hand, it was a question of nipping round to the shops after Monday morning band call and trying on the charm. It was noticeable that girl dancers tended to get better cuts of meat than the men in the company – but then the men weren't bothered with any quid pro quo with the local butcher's boy subsequently.

Sex was notable by its absence in my touring days – not *complete* absence, you understand, but comparative absence, and I'm sure that many jugglers married their assistants not out of lust or even necessity but because two really could live as cheaply as one on the road, and if you were married your partner got housekeeping rather than a salary. I had one brief, chaste romance with a landlady's daughter in Blyth, Northumberland, and another, fractionally less chaste, with a young lady in Leeds, by the name of Roberta. A year or two after my last performance on a music-hall bill at the City Varieties (a theatre subsequently made famous by Barney Colehan's TV series, *The Good Old Days*) I returned to Leeds in the pre-London tour of a West End revue, *For Adults Only*. On the Tuesday evening I was told there was someone to see me at the stage door. It was Roberta with a baby in her arms! Not mine, folks. In the interim she'd married an American serviceman, borne his son and had come to say goodbye before

leaving for Missouri. I capered through that evening's performance with a light heart.

The worst digs I ever had, not counting the bed-sitter in Derby where I was charged fifteen shillings (75p) for the week, were in St Helens, where the landlady had been looking after 'pros' for over forty years. The 'remarks' book where former lodgers had scribbled their comments wasn't too encouraging, but she was an obliging old soul who insisted on doing my washing. However, she half dried my white shirts in front of the coal fire in the draughty kitchen and ironed in the flakes of ash with which they'd become spotted. As a result they were ingrained with grey smuts ever after and looked as if they were suffering from an unmentionable disease. But at least I had a room on my own, although she'd asked me whether, if she reduced the rent, I'd share with 'another gentleman'. I refused, preferring to pay the extra five shillings. 'Oh,' she said, 'I had *Soldiers In Skirts* last week — and they didn't mind sharing at all.'

Playing With Shakespeare

IN 1962 I was with the Royal Shakespeare Company at Stratford-upon-Avon acting as an extra. It was a twelve-hour day, what with rehearsals and matinées, and a six-day week, most of which I spent filling a large gap in the stage (I'm 6′4½″) as a lord, soldier or servant, clutching banners or spears – reacting rather than acting – and bearing bits of furniture and props on and off the stage. All this for £11 a week, which rose at the end of the season to £13 a week and five words in Scofield's *King Lear* – 'Edmund is dead, my lord' – which gets put down peevishly by Albany with: 'That's but a trifle here!'

We had some fun at Stratford, with Shakespeare's words among other things. In rehearsing *Macbeth* Eric Porter would respond to Donalbain's query – 'What is amiss?' – with a camp inflection: '*You* are! And do not *know* it.' Then there was – 'With an indissoluble tie, for ever, *nit!*' Being a servant in Shakespeare was no great shakes in this and other respects, unless you had a line or two to spotlight your humble presence. Some could be stunners. In fact the most ghastly one-liner in Shakespeare must be in *Richard II*, when a most sinister Servant tells the horrified Duke of York: 'An hour before I came, the Duchess died . . .'

At Stratford I lodged in a small terrace house in Chestnut Walk for £3.10 a week, plus breakfast. This usually consisted of leathery fried eggs, cereal, tea, and tablets of toast, served in a cramped back room, where the other lodger and I, as well as the landlady and her aged mother, would sit in moody silence around the breakfast table consuming our comestibles. There might be comments about the weather or some local event; or the other lodger, always a man, would quote from the *Mirror* or the *Express*. But the Theatre and the plays, which were of all-consuming interest to me, were rarely mentioned. The aged person grunted and sniffed. She glared and muttered but seldom spoke, only addressing me once, accusingly – 'You don't say much, *do* you?'

Her daughter had long, flowing, fairish tresses – like an ageing Ophelia, I thought. Her eyebrows were pencilled arcs and her cheeks were rouged. Round-eyed, she padded about the back parlour in her dressing-gown, subservient to every demand of the weird old woman wrapped in wool. The house was dark, the dull rooms dwarfed by large and looming Victorian furniture. I had a bulky double bed in my first floor room at the front, but as its length was less than mine, I lay across it. I was never in, unless to sleep. If not rehearsing or performing, I would be out consorting with others in the cast in the town, meeting for coffee, or at a pub, and returning late at night, after a performance, from the actors' favoured hostelry, *The Dirty Duck*. I would let myself in with my key, over-carefully, and creep upstairs, dimly shadowed by a ceiling light, avoiding the baleful eyes of a big stuffed cat that crouched in a glass case on a cabinet on the stairs.

Sometimes I was asked to vacate my room; it was needed by special visitors. Who were they? When I was away, did all the inmates form a coven and dance naked at night around the Rollright Stones? Back in my room, that seemed even colder and darker, I would lie diagonally on the box-like bed, hearing the odd creaks and whispers within the house (presumably from the furniture and plumbing) and wonder that Ophelia and her ancient mother were up to in their secret rooms. I always locked my bedroom door.

Please Note

S OME of the notices written and displayed by landladies in theatrical digs are legendary. They formed a literature, even a language, of their own. Here are few memorable examples – once seen never forgotten.

Please Note
ALL FOREIGN COINS PLACED IN THE GAS METER WILL BE PROSECUTED

Please Note
PAYMENT MUST BE MADE BY FRIDAY LUNCHTIME OR SATURDAY AT THE VERY LATEST OR LUGGAGE MAY BE CONFISTICATED BUT PREFERABLY FRIDAY

Important Notice
NO POLITICS *NO RELIGION OR FRIENDS IN AFTER 11pm*

Meals
BREAKFAST 8.00–9.00. SUNDAY 9.15. EXCEPT ON EASTER SUNDAY OR WHEN CHRISTMAS FALLS ON A SUNDAY, BECAUSE IT INTERFERES

Please Note
THERE'S A CHAMBER POT UNDER THE BED. IF USED DURING THE NIGHT DO NOT REPLACE UNDER THE BED, AS THE STEAM RUSTS THE SPRINGS